COAT OF MANY COLORS

By
Barrie Stavis

Plays
Harpers Ferry
The Man Who Never Died
Lamp at Midnight
Refuge

Fiction
Home, Sweet Home!
The Chain of Command

COAT OF MANY COLORS

A Play About Joseph in Egypt

by

BARRIE STAVIS

INTRODUCTION BY
JOHN LEWIN

South Brunswick
New York: A.S. Barnes and Company
London: Thomas Yoseloff Ltd

A. S. Barnes and Co., Inc.
Cranbury, New Jersey 08512

Thomas Yoseloff Ltd
18 Charing Cross Road
London W.C. 2, England

6819
Printed in the United States of America

FOR BERNICE, FOR ADELAIDE BEAN,
AND FOR
BEN IRVING, WHO DIED BEFORE HIS TIME.

CONTENTS

Acknowledgments   7
Introduction, by John Lewin   11
Production Notes   19
Cast of Characters   21
COAT OF MANY COLORS
Act I — Scene 1   25
        Scene 2   46
        Scenc 3   61
Act II — Scene 1   87
        Scene 2   105
        Scene 3   132

ACKNOWLEDGMENTS

First and foremost a deep and grateful bow to Adelaide Bean, colleague and cherished friend. We went through an exhilarating process as new vistas opened up. Her criticism and advice were invaluable, helping me to achieve new insights with the material.

Special thanks to Dr. Harold I. Hansen and to Douglas Campbell. Their work and advice were of inestimable value in helping me mold the play into final shape.

Many other people generously gave of their time and talent as the play went through successive drafts. Thanks again to my two staunch friends and advisers, B. J. Whiting and Stephen Gray. And my thanks also to Dr. Alexander Thomas, Dr. Stella Chess, Dr. John Reich, Prof. John F. Matthews, Prof. Christian H. Moe, the late Ben Irving, Raymond Bechtle, Dr. Sam Smiley, Prof. Mordecai Gorelik, Prof. Richard Schechner, Gordon Rogoff, Hy Kalus, Dr. Howard Selsam, David Dannenbaum, Morton Stavis, Esther Stavis, Joseph K. Reichbart, Ruth Reichbart, Richard Reichbart, Joseph K. Rider, Dr. Reuben Silver, Dr. Juris M. Svendsen, Dr. Allan Lewis, Ralph Al-

ACKNOWLEDGMENTS

swang, Arthur Levine, Dr. Lael J. Woodbury, Dr. Charles Henson, Dr. Charles W. Whitman, Beverly Warner, Robert Struthers, Dr. Robert I. Schneideman, Boris Tumarin, Berta Tumarin, Lily Turner, Lawrence Weinberg, William Greene and Sir Tyrone Guthrie.

And, finally—as always—for my wife, Bernice. Her integrity and patience are formidable; her perception and taste, uncanny.

B. S.

INTRODUCTION

Joseph's first appearance in this play has all the trappings of the miraculous—to such a melodramatic extent in fact, as to introduce at once a fine note of irony and paradox on which Barrie Stavis rings the full changes in the course of the drama. Gad, one of Joseph's older brothers who is in the fields tending the flock, challenges Jehovah to show his power by meeting a simple human need, an ever present concern of desert people—the need for water. A flash storm arises on cue drenching the brothers and ending with the showman's flourish of a rainbow, out of which steps Joseph in his coat of many colors. Shortly, Joseph comes up with a human solution for the water shortage—dig a reservoir. Ah! we exclaim—man's reason; the noblest work of God. And when Joseph self-righteously declares himself Jehovah's anointed, our thought is confirmed.

But somehow we are irresistibly reminded of the impressive demonstration of Zeus in Sartre's *The Flies,* leading to the conclusion that only through submission to the Divine Will (as interpreted through the authority of

11

priest and ruler) can man find peace. And there comes
to mind Orestes' assessment of the human position as he
challenges Zeus: "Outside nature, against nature, without
excuse, beyond remedy, except what remedy I find writ-
ten within myself. But I shall not return under your law;
I am doomed to have no other law but mine. Nor shall I
come back to nature, the nature you found good; in it are
a thousand beaten paths all leading up to you—but I must
blaze my trail." And Orestes continues the challenge to
Zeus: "For I, Zeus, am a man, and every man must find
out his own way." [*The Flies* by Jean-Paul Sartre, in NO
EXIT and Three Other Plays, New York, Vintage Books,
1955, P. 122.]

Joseph himself comes around to the realization that he
must blaze his own trail, that "every man must find out
his own way." But he will arrive at this understanding
only after his years in Egypt when, as a man of "God-
given" wisdom and charismatic presence, he nevertheless
allies himself with the Power Establishment of Pharaoh
and priest in the mistaken notion that ultimately his
work and purpose can be accomplished through them.

Joseph's human reason possesses him to a degree un-
precedented in an age dominated by the terrors of the
unconscious and of a world of nature seemingly controlled
only by magical propitiation of its all-powerful and inscrutable God (or gods). His mind cuts through the web
of superstitious fears, awakening admiration, attraction
and unease in those, like Vashnee, Arraffi and Pharaoh,
who are perceptive enough to comprehend the wisdom
of human solutions to human problems, but are too bound

by vested interest in the superstition-supported Order of Authority to admit that *all solutions must be human.*

Joseph is never in really grave danger of selling his integrity to the Egyptian Establishment, though he must become part of it to attain his rational and liberating objectives. He must take advantage of the cynicism of Pharaoh and Vashnee by outshining them with his own shrewdness; hence, to an extent, he may strike the superficial observer, unaware of what it means for a displaced person to survive in a hostile land, as the prototype of the Clever Jew. But in Barrie Stavis' play, the fact that Joseph is a Hebrew is irrelevant to the main lines of struggle between him on the one hand, and the Pharaoh and the Egyptian priesthood on the other. (If the essence of Joseph lies in his being a Hebrew, then every innovator in history who foresaw the possibility of controlling nature for man's purposes must be considered Hebrew! For though he is of the genus of Spinoza, of Marx, of Freud, he was equally of the genus of a Democritus and a Galileo; the visions of truth of all of these men were anathema to the establishments of their times.) As for the Establishment, they use the fact that Joseph is a Hebrew to destroy him only when it is necessary to preserve their power— as they would attack any other outsider who no longer served their purposes and who had even become dangerous to them.

In describing Pharaoh and Vashnee as cynics, we point to their credo that man exists to be manipulated; and they are well aware that this manipulation is not for the good of the manipulated, but for the good of themselves, the manipulators. The cynic sees the mass of men forever

13

blind to their own potential. Joseph, on the other hand, has faith in man's ability to find his own way if the blinders are removed; he desires, in short, for all men to be heroes as *he* is a hero. Whether this desire is illusory in man's present stage of development remains to be seen, but if it is an illusion it is the noblest of all illusions.

Joseph's great vision is shattered on the means-end rock on which so many social reformers have come to grief. He makes the fatal mistake of adopting the methods of the cynical Establishment, of manipulating men for his own ends, though these ends will be good for the very people he drives. The workers whom he has put to forced labor on his nature-taming project will not allow themselves to be enslaved "even for their own good." Joseph attempts to remove the blinders; he tells the workers the truth. But because he had worked apart from and above them, because he had used inhuman means even though for an idealistic goal, because he had never helped prepare them for the truth, the very people for whom his work would mean ultimate freedom, turn against him. The truth he advances to them, they reject—along with the task he had saddled upon them. Indeed, without adequate preparation, the truth as well as the task would appear to them as parts of the same intolerable burden.

Joseph's truth, though rejected, defies priestly authority, threatening the destruction of its powers and privileges: the ritual, the caste system, to say nothing of the economic gain. The result is predictable, and comes about, ironically, because of the great projects initiated by Joseph which have so enhanced the power of the Pharaoh and the priesthood. It is this very power they now exercise against him. He is sent to his death in the desert and to the company of martyrs to truth and human freedom. It is around such martyrs that Barrie Stavis has constructed his powerful tetralogy of which this is the final play.

Of Stavis' four heroes, Galileo Galilei *(Lamp at Midnight)*, Joe Hill *(The Man Who Never Died)*, John Brown *(Harpers Ferry)*, and Joseph in this play, it is Joseph who has the most incisive and independent intelligence, coupled with a wry humor and an audacious common sense. (When, as a slave during his first years in Egypt, Joseph is thrown into a dungeon for insubordination, he prays to Jehovah for deliverance in this manner: "It is not entirely my fault that I am here. A good part of it—I am not saying how much—is Your fault, too. Please, don't get angry with me. Facts are facts, Jehovah, and the fact is that You gave me the brain I have and You surely gave it to me to use. It's this brain of mine, the one *You* gave me, that's getting me into trouble.") This humor and audacity enables Stavis to make considerably greater use of wit and comic detachment than heretofore without mitigating the force of this play of ideas, of which form he is one of the great living masters.

John Lewin
March, 1968

15

The play takes place in ancient Canaan and Egypt.

ACT I

Scene 1: The Plains of Dothan in Canaan. A few thousand years ago.

Scene 2: A dungeon in Potiphar's palace in Egypt. Three years later.

Scene 3: Joseph's room in Potiphar's palace. Two years later.

ACT II

Scene 1: The Throne Room in Pharaoh's palace. Two years later.

Scene 2: Joseph's office. Ten years later.

Scene 3: Site of Dam Number Four near the Nile River. Ten weeks later.

PRODUCTION NOTES

DESIGN OF THE SET: The set is to be extremely simple. The play is to be performed on a stage consisting of open playing areas. These playing areas can be obtained by platforms, steps or levels of different heights situated in various parts of the stage. In one scene a platform or level can be used as a room in Potiphar's palace while in another it can serve as the headquarters of the dam area near the Nile.

MUSIC: Music is an important part of the production of this work. Musical possibilities are indicated in the script.

CAST OF CHARACTERS

REUBEN	*Oldest son of Jacob, borne by Leah.*
SIMEON	*Second son of Jacob, borne by Leah.*
LEVI	*Third son of Jacob, borne by Leah.*
JUDAH	*Fourth son of Jacob, borne by Leah.*
DAN	*Fifth son of Jacob, borne by Bilhah.*
NAPHTALI	*Sixth son of Jacob, borne by Bilhah.*
GAD	*Seventh son of Jacob, borne by Zilpah.*
ASHER	*Eighth son of Jacob, borne by Zilpah.*
ISSACHER	*Ninth son of Jacob, borne by Leah.*
ZEBULUN	*Tenth son of Jacob, borne by Leah.*
JOSEPH	*Eleventh son of Jacob, borne by Rachel.*
AN ISHMAELITE SLAVE MERCHANT	
ARRAFFI	*Chamberlain to Potiphar.*
VASHNEE	*Wife to Potiphar.*
POTIPHAR	*Governor of Egypt.*
MALFI	*Joseph's first assistant.*
PRINCESS ASENATH	*Daughter of Potiphar and Vashnee.*
PHARAOH	*King of Egypt.*
SHARSHEES	*Pharaoh's wine bearer.*
TWO ENGINEERS	
A WARRIOR	

Guards, Slaves, Soothsayers, Workers.

21

COAT OF MANY COLORS

'Heroes need no gods and no tyrants.''

ACT I

Scene 1

A few thousand years ago. The plains of Dothan in Canaan.

The stage is in semi-darkness except for a spotlight which picks up Reuben on the side of the stage. He is playing on a shepherd's pipe. It is the Water theme. He plays for a few moments, then speaks directly to the audience.

REUBEN. I am Reuben, the eldest son of Jacob. *(The lights begin to come up. It is late afternoon. The sun is sinking beyond the horizon. There is a well . . . .Ten shepherds are preparing their evening meal. These men are the first ten sons of Jacob: Reuben, Simeon, Levi, Judah, Dan, Naphtali, Gad, Asher, Issacher and Zebulun. They wear simple shepherd's robes and sandals. The brothers continue their tasks in pantomime as Reuben says:)* These are my brothers. *(Points to two of them who are making a fireplace of stones.)* Those two—Simeon and Levi. My full brothers. *(Points to two others. One is cutting off chunks of meat with a knife, the other is helping by holding the carcass.)* The two at the meat for our evening meal are Judah and Issacher. Also my full brothers. *(Points to a brother who has come in with some sticks and twigs for the fire.)* Zebulun. He, too, my full brother. We six are the sons of Leah. *(Points to two others.)* Dan and Naphtali, working at the sheepskin, my half-brothers. They were borne by Bilhah, my father's second wife. *(Points to two others.)* Gad and Asher bringing stones to the fireplace, my half-brothers. They were born by Zilpah, my father's third wife. . . . We have another brother, a half-brother; his name is Joseph. The youngest. The only son of Rachel, my father's favorite wife—as Joseph is my father's favorite son. Joseph, the favorite, is not here. He's never with us. He lives in the tents. Stays at home with the father. The favorite son of the favorite wife.

You should know that we ten sons of Jacob have been out on the plains for many weeks; that we cannot find good pasture; that we have searched for grass and water from the day we left for the fields, not finding them our flock is in poor condition; that we are tired; that our tempers are surly; that this is the end of a day when many things have gone wrong. *(Turns to the brothers.)* Gad! Look out! *(Moves into the scene. From here on he is no longer the Narrator, but one of the brothers.)*

GAD. *(Has been lifting a large stone near the mouth of the well. He drops the stone and springs aside. Then He creeps up cautiously to the place where the stone was lying and seizes a snake deftly by the back of its neck. He holds it up.)* Ha! Tried to spike me on the leg, did you?

ZEBULUN. Mash its head and throw it into the well before it snags you.

26

GAD. I wasn't born yesterday, brother. I know how to handle a snake. *(Draws his knife, cuts off the snake's head and flips it into the well. To Simeon.)* When do we eat?

SIMEON. You can have it now if you want it raw.

LEVI. Is this all we get, the lean carcass of one little flea-bitten sheep?

SIMEON. I cook all I'm allowed. The father says we stuff ourselves and starve the flock.

LEVI. If a man works he's got to eat, and I expect to eat my fill.

NAPHTALI. What does he think we have for bellies—little bags like Joseph's?

ZEBULUN. Somebody ought to tell him we're grown men.

JUDAH. Was it last night or the night before that your mother rocked you in your cradle to stop your squalling?

ZEBULUN. I'll crack your skull.

JUDAH. *(Mockingly.)* I remember—you once killed a flea. *(Zebulun rushes toward Judah.)*

ISSACHER. *(Stands between them.)* Fool! How many times have I told you, if you must fight you have half-brothers.

ZEBULUN. Make him keep his tongue off me. *(Glares at Judah, then angrily strides to the well and spits in it.)*

ASHER. *(Breaking the tension.)* There's a three-month-old lamb out there. What do you say, brothers, shall I get him? *(There is a chorus of approval. Asher starts off.)*

REUBEN. *(Detaining Asher.)* No!

LEVI. *(To Asher.)* There are no Josephs here. Go fetch

27

the lamb. *(Asher goes off. The brothers waiting for Asher's return sink on the ground in the listless positions of weary men.)*

SIMEON. The day we left the tents Joseph started his wild talk about dreams again. He came to me at dawn and told me he had a dream about how to find water underground. Jehovah came to him in a dream and—

ZEBULUN. The next time he tries to tell me one of his dreams, I'll cut his tongue out.

JUDAH. *(Mockingly, as before.)* Yes, I remember—you once killed a flea.

ZEBULUN. *(Also sprawled on the ground, too weary to move.)* And I'll kill another. *(The brothers join in a derisive chorus of ba-a-aas.)*

GAD. Does Joseph really have those dreams with Jehovah appearing in them all the time?

REUBEN. Maybe some of them he makes up—but the others are real. Anything can happen in a dream. So why shouldn't Jehovah appear in the dreams of Joseph?

GAD. If Jehovah is so busy marching around in the dreams of Joseph, when does He have time to visit all the other people?

DAN. Why does Jehovah pick only Joseph? Why doesn't Jehovah visit one of us in a dream?

ZEBULUN. Because he's a favorite. The favorite son of the favorite wife. He's even Jehovah's favorite.

LEVI. Where is Asher with that lamb? I'm hungry.

GAD. *(To Reuben, who has begun to play on his shepherd's pipe.)* What are you playing?

28

REUBEN. What a river sounds like.

GAD. Running river. Water music. I would settle for twenty drops of water from that sky.

SIMEON. From Yassid to Basha, from Basha to Shechem, from Shechem to Dothan.

ISSACHER. We have driven the flock and driven ourselves. What have we to show for it?

REUBEN. *(Looking down into the well.)* This well never ran dry before.

GAD. *(Spits into it with disgust.)* A slimy pit.

SIMEON. The father will be angry with us.

GAD. Let the father be angry with Jehovah. It's Jehovah's job to supply pasture and water. We've looked for it.

SIMEON. The father will be angry not with Jehovah, but with us.

GAD. *(With slowly mounting energy gets to his knees and calls out to the sky.)* Jehovah, why are You so stingy with Your water? We have prayed to You; we have sacrificed to You. We've held to our share of the bargain; why don't You hold to Yours, You stingy cheat of a Jehovah?

REUBEN. *(Stops his playing for a moment.)* I'd be careful if I were you.

GAD. *(Rises to his feet. His energy grows. He loses all caution and shouts wildly to the sky.)* Twenty drops of water is all I ask, damn You. Twenty drops. *(A pause)* Come on, Jehovah—twenty drops. *(A pause.)* Jehovah, I think You're a fraud. You couldn't deliver twenty drops of water even if You wanted to.

29

SIMEON. *(Who is sprawled on the ground, face to the sky.)* That cloud. It wasn't there a moment ago.

REUBEN. *(Looks up at the cloud and then looks quizzically at Gad.)* No bigger than a hand. The hand of Jehovah?

SIMEON. It is coming toward us.

ZEBELUN. And it is getting bigger.

SIMEON. Look! It covers the sky. *(The lights grow dark and ominous. There is a low rumble and then a lashing, terrible torrent hits the brothers. Note: There is not to be actual rain. The effect is to be achieved by a combination of lights and sound, and, perhaps, by the additional use of a projection screen, or a translucency of film thrown from a motion picture projector.)*

GAD. Jehovah! Dear, sweet, kind Jehovah, I only asked for twenty drops just to see if You could deliver. But not this.

REUBEN. That will teach you to challenge Jehovah.

GAD. It's your fault, Reuben. Why did you play that water music? *(It is a flash storm of dry countries and it is over in a minute. The sky is clear again. The brothers huddle up, drenched, cold and miserable. A rainbow appears.)*

SIMEON. Look! A rainbow.

GAD. *(In anger to the brothers.)* After soaking and chilling us to the bone, He sends a rainbow.

SIMEON. Don't aggravate Him. You can never tell what He'll do next if He gets aggravated.

GAD. It's me that's aggravated.

30

SIMEON. Let's take the soaking as though we liked it. Otherwise, who knows what He'll do to us.

GAD. It's the rainbow—that's what aggravates me. A rainbow is the covenant of friendship between Jehovah and us. And for Him to send down a rainbow after the soaking He gave us—He's unfair.

SIMEON. Ssshhhh. He'll hear you.

GAD. Let Him.

REUBEN. Jehovah is all-powerful. Beware of His wrath.

GAD. Let Jehovah beware of me. I have a weapon against Him.

DAN. What weapon can you have against Jehovah?

GAD. The weapon of silence.

REUBEN. (*His face takes on an expression of horror. He addresses the sky.*) I beg You, Jehovah, pay no heed to him. His rage feeds on our frustration.

GAD. (*During the following, Reuben begins to play loudly, but Gad's voice rises to overcome the continually rising volume of the flute so that toward the end of his speech, He is shouting.*) Jehovah is all-powerful? Jehovah sits on high, enthroned and majestic? Jehovah is known, is mighty, because we give Him honor and declare Him mighty. And what if we here, together, now, make a pact to keep our silence about Jehovah? We sons of Jacob, stemming from the seed of Abraham, Isaac and Jacob, are the only ones in the world who worship Jehovah. If we keep silence, say not a single word about Him, what good would it do Him then, to sit up there enthroned and majestic, alone, ignored, with no one knowing Him, with

31

no one to worship Him, with no one to sing His praises or His might? So let Him be careful how He treats us in the future. *(Reuben is winded from his blowing, Gad from his shouting. They have to rest, breathing heavily. Simeon cuts into the charged silence.)*

SIMEON. I think that rainbow is moving.

JUDAH. It's a man. Stepping out of the end of the rainbow.

SIMEON. Look how he holds his fine coat as he steps over the sheep dung.

DAN. By the Lord, Jehovah, it's the coat of many colors.

ZEBULUN. Joseph! The father sent him to spy on us.

DAN. That's a fine coat.

ZEBULUN. But it should have more red in it. Let's dye it for him, brothers. *(A shrill whistle is heard as Joseph approaches.)*

REUBEN. I'll answer him. *(Puts his fingers to his mouth.)*

ZEBULUN. *(Stopping him.)* No. *(As the brothers look at him questioningly.)* Let's hide. When he comes, we'll jump him and give him a beating.

REUBEN. What's he done to you?

DAN. He has the coat of many colors.

ISSACHER. He's the favorite of the father.

ZEBULUN. *(Dragging Reuben off by the arm.)* Hurry. Here he comes. *(The others quickly follow Zebulun and Reuben. There is quiet for a moment. Then Joseph walks on wearing the coat of many colors. This is a cloak pieced together with strips of primitively splendid material. It*

32

stands out sharply against the drab robes of his brothers. Joseph is eighteen years old, above medium height. Lacking his brothers' burly strength, he possesses a lithe, taut quality of mind and body.

He surveys the scene before him, puzzled. He sees the chunks of meat and fingers them hungrily; peers into the well and moves away with a grimace; starts to wipe his hands on his coat, but remembers and wipes them carefully on his undergarment. He is tired; He throws himself on the ground. Something attracts his attention and he studies the ground intently.

Gad, Simeon, Naphtali and Zebulun enter silently. They beckon the others to surround Joseph. As they approach, Joseph becomes aware of their presence. Instantly he is on the alert without letting them know. At a signal from Zebulun, they are about to pounce on him with sticks in their hands, but without turning to face them, Joseph cries out.)

JOSEPH. Welcome, brothers. *(The brothers stop short, glaring at him foolishly.)*

ZEBULUN. Welcome—Ba-a-a-a-aa! *(There are ba-a-aas from some and snorts of disgust from others.)*

DAN. What were you doing there, crawling on the ground in your fine coat?

JOSEPH. Watching two tribes of ants. Thousands of them fighting their greatest battle while we above know their world is only a few grains of sand. *(Zebulun steps on the ants, crushing them.)*

SIMEON. What do you want here?

JOSEPH. Most of all, something to eat.

SIMEON. You didn't come all the way from the tents just to eat.

JOSEPH. The father sent me to bring him news of you and the flock.

ZEBULUN. You mean the father sent you to spy on us.

GAD. Is the father becoming an old grasshopper that he sends the great, strong Joseph to mind his ten little brothers?

LEVI. Having a good time at home alone with all the women servants, Joseph?

JOSEPH. *(Shyly, but with dignity.)* You know that I don't.

ZEBULUN. It's your own fault. Surely the wenches are willing enough.

JUDAH. He doesn't even *dream* what he's missing.

SIMEON. Don't get him started on his dreams again.

ZEBULUN. Take care, Joseph. The world is full of wicked women.

GAD. Some day one of them will catch you and turn that fine coat over your head—and you'll never be the same again.

SIMEON. Maybe that'll stop his dreams. He'll have something real to think about.

JOSEPH. *(Embarrassed, examines the meat)* Will the meat be ready soon? I haven't eaten since sunrise yesterday.

DAN. The father wouldn't send you away without bread in your sack.

JOSEPH. I've been following you from place to place. No wonder the flocks look lean and mangy.

ZEBULUN. Is that the report you will carry back to the father?

JOSEPH. I must tell the truth. They *are* lean and the land *is* dry and barren. Even that well—there's nothing in it but slime. . . . There should be some way to collect water and hold it in one place. Then when it's dry, we could use it.

ZEBULUN. Like a lake, huh?

JOSEPH. *(Seizing on Zebulun's idea.)* Yes! That's it. Like a lake. That storm we had a moment ago. All that water that came down from the skies—what good did it do? And where is it now? Just a few puddles on the ground.

ZEBULUN. Digging a lake is a big job.

JOSEPH. I will tell you how to do it.

GAD. Oh. We do the work and you take charge?

JOSEPH. I know how.

DAN. You rule us? You will be the master? That's the way it's to be?

JOSEPH. It will be for your own good! You'll bless me for it.

GAD. Another of your wild dreams, Joseph.

JOSEPH. *(To Reuben.)* You understand, Reuben. You know what I mean, don't you?

REUBEN. *(Takes Joseph aside so that they are not heard by the others. Reproaching him.)* You shouldn't talk this way to your brothers.

JOSEPH. I thought you understood—

REUBEN. Do you understand your brothers? You've

35

never once been out in the fields with us. Baked by the sun in the day, frozen by the wind at night. And always the search for grass and water—

JOSEPH. But that's why I just said—

REUBEN. Do you know what we've been through this past month? And then you come from your easy life in the tents with your bright ideas—but we are the men who do the work.

JOSEPH. I thought you were on my side, Reuben—

REUBEN. I am.

JOSEPH. Why can't they love me for myself? I can do so many good things for them.

REUBEN. Until you've worked with us, until you know on your back what a shepherd's life is like, you will be alone—and alone you can't carry out your plans. Your *ideas* might be good, but they will fall on deaf ears. They will die—or be fought by us.

GAD. (*His anger has been mounting. Now he cuts in on Joseph and Reuben.*) Listen, brothers. I've had a dream too—it must run in the family. While he was talking, I dreamt I picked him up, fine feathers and all, and dropped him into that slimy well with the other worms.

DAN. A good place for him.

JOSEPH. (*Alarmed, pleading.*) You're jesting. You wouldn't harm me, brothers. (*With conviction.*) Besides, Jehovah wouldn't let me be cast into the pit.

ASHER. (*Entering with a dead lamb on his shoulders.*) Here it is, brothers. Meat. Soft and sweet.

JOSEPH. (*Touches the lamb. Innocently unaware.*) It is

36

still warm. Did some wild beast attack the flock and kill it? *(Joseph understands that the lamb has been slaughtered. Virtuously, with a quality of offensive priggishness.)* The father has forbidden you to kill the lambs. And he's right. We must think of the future. I have not eaten for two days, but I wouldn't touch such flesh.

ZEBULUN. *(Maliciously.)* He thinks we're going to cram it down his throat!

LEVI. You won't touch any meat here. The father sent you for news of us. Go back and tell him we eat heartily, but we have no food for talebearers.

JOSEPH. I can't go back without food. It's three days journey. *(Silence. He looks from brother to brother.)* I'm hungry. Give me food before I go.

GAD. You'll go as you came—with your belly empty.

ZEBULUN. Let's give him a few clouts to send him off.

JOSEPH. *(Now frightened, speaks with bravado.)* How dare you try to harm the blessed one of this generation?

GAD. Blessed ram's tail! I now see we're going to have to throw you into that well.

JOSEPH. All ten of you couldn't put me in that pit.

REUBEN. Joseph, don't!

ZEBULUN. Watch the stars fly out of this fist of mine. *(They close in on Joseph. Gad seizes him by the collar of his coat.)*

JOSEPH. *(Visibly summoning up his courage.)* Stop! I am Jehovah's anointed!

GAD. *(Holding the collar. Shakes Joseph roughly.)* Oh! Jehovah's anointed!

JOSEPH. Yes.

GAD. What did he anoint you with—a cow pile? Keep your mouth shut or you'll get another. *(Reuben places himself between Joseph and his brothers, protecting Joseph.)*

JOSEPH. *(Speaks impressively.)* Jehovah visited Abraham, the great grandfather, and Isaac, the grandfather—

REUBEN. *(Cutting in.)* Keep quiet. You talk too much.

JOSEPH. *(Rushing on.)* —And Jacob, the father, and so magnified Himself. But through me, Jehovah shall excel Himself! *(The assurance with which he says this impresses the brothers. They all stand still with the exception of Gad.)*

GAD. Well, it's not fair to make Him do all the visiting. You should visit Him. You'll find Him at the bottom of that well.

JOSEPH. *(Staring directly into their eyes, especially Gad's.)* I know that I shall find Him in the pit. He is everywhere. And He is watching you—all of you—this very moment. *(The brothers shift positions uncomfortably, Joseph watches them closely.)*

GAD. Bah! More of his wild talk. He's been having another dream. *(He advances slowly on Joseph, but the other brothers do not follow him.)*

JOSEPH. *(His voice takes on a deeper timbre. He speaks with great conviction.)* Yes, I had a dream. I had this dream last night. We were in the wheat fields binding the sheaves. Suddenly my sheaf moved as if it were alive. I shook it and it shone with a golden glow. Then it rose and stood upright. Your sheaves saw and trembled. Then they gathered round and bowed unto my golden sheaf.

GAD. Are you sure none of them gave yours a kick on the bottom?

JOSEPH. *(Holding his ground.)* I had yet another dream last night.

REUBEN. *(Quietly to Joseph, so that the others cannot hear.)* Joseph, stop. One dream is enough. Don't spoil it. Go quickly.

JOSEPH. *(Half in despair, half the gambler risking all.)* I can't stop! I have to go on! *(Again his voice takes on a deep timbre as he looks off into space as though transfigured by a vision.)* In this second dream, the great red sun came and bowed to me. Then came the silver moon and bowed to me. Then came the eleven great stars and bowed to me. And I had kind words for them all. *(Looks searchingly into the faces of his brothers.)* Brothers, do you know the meaning of these two dreams? *(The spell is broken. The brothers begin to stir uneasily and in mounting anger.)*

GAD. *(In a great shout of rage.)* They mean only one thing to you, Joseph. *(To the brothers.)* Come on.

DAN. Into the pit with him. *(Two of the brothers step in quickly and grab Reuben's arms. They yank him aside so that he is no longer able to stand between Joseph and the brothers. At the same time Gad and Dan seize Joseph in preparation for the well. Gad claps his hand over Joseph's mouth.)*

REUBEN. *(Tries to break away but does not succeed.*

39

Cries out from the side, where he is firmly held.) Jehovah will be angry with us.

GAD. We're throwing him into the pit—that's our business. If Jehovah wants to fish him out—that's His.

DAN. Pull off his coat. We'll keep it. *(Joseph bites Gad's hand. Gad bites Joseph's hand. Joseph cries out in pain, thus releasing Gad's hand.)*

GAD. Two can bite as well as one.

JOSEPH. Brothers, Jehovah *did* visit me—I *am* destined.

GAD. You're destined for the well, Joseph. *(Zebulun stuffs Joseph's mouth. Reuben tries to break loose. Two more brothers hold him, so that he is helpless.)*

GAD. *(As he and Zebulun swing Joseph rhythmically by the arms and legs.)* One for luck—

ZEBULUN. And two for the show.

GAD. Make it three—

ALL. *(In chorus.)* And let him go! *(They drop Joseph into the well. He utters a piercing cry of terror. The brothers who have been holding Reuben, now release him. He watches sorrowfully.)*

GAD. *(Peers over the rim and calls mockingly.)* Hey, Joseph, did you find Jehovah down there—or was He off visiting some other blessed bull's calf?

JOSEPH. Save me, brothers. This pit is filled with snakes.

GAD. Only a nest of harmless vipers. Speak kindly to them and they'll rise up and bow to you.

DAN. Careful, Gad!

GAD. *(Snatches the snake by the back of its neck, draws*

his knife and severs its head, then calls down into the well.) Hey, king—ruler of men—here's a rope to haul yourself out. *(Throws the dead snake into the pit. Joseph cries out in terror.)*

ZEBULUN. What's the matter, Prince—did your hand slip?

GAD. Have Jehovah turn your coat into a rainbow and climb up it with a bag of gold.

JOSEPH. Jehovah *will* come. I know He will. *(Jangling bells are heard in the distance.)*

GAD. Here He comes now.

ZEBULUN. Jehovah?

GAD. Yes. Don't you hear Him? *(Some of the brothers are shaken and impressed. Then, seeing the cause for the bells, are themselves once more.)*

LEVI. *(Looking off in the distance.)* A caravan.

NAPHTALI. Traders going down to Egypt.

ZEBULUN. I'd give a year of my life to go with them.

GAD. It would cost you more than that if their slave drivers ever got you in their clutches.

ZEBULUN. I know a good end for a prince.

SIMEON. The well is good enough for me.

DAN. Zebulun's idea is better. We would be rid of him without having his blood on our hands.

ASHER. And get paid for him besides.

REUBEN. He is our blood. You cannot sell your own blood.

41

GAD. *(Brushing Reuben aside.)* Quick, Dan, haul him out. *(Dan picks up a coil of rope.)*

REUBEN. Not the well and not slavery. He's learned his lesson. Haul him out and send him home. There'll be no more trouble from him.

GAD. Listen, Reuben, my half-brother, that well is big enough for two. And two can be sold for slaves as well as one.

JUDAH. *(Comes between Gad and Reuben and cries out.)* Sons of Leah! *(Immediately Simeon, Levi, Issacher and Zebulun join him, forming a protective ring around Reuben.)*

REUBEN. *(Bitterly.)* If Joseph had full brothers to protect him, would he be in the pit now? *(The six brothers stand against the four. Then an Ishmaelite slave driver appears. He carries a whip.)*

THE ISHMAELITE. Hail, sons of Abraham!

GAD. Hail. What is your tribe?

THE ISHMAELITE. Your servant is an Ishmaelite.

GAD. Which way do you travel?

THE ISHMAELITE. Into Egypt.

GAD. And your merchandise?

THE ISHMAELITE. Spices and slaves.

GAD. Slaves. Would you buy another—young, strong and well-fed? *(Two of the brothers hold Reuben firmly.)*

THE ISHMAELITE. At a good price.

GAD. Fifty pieces of silver?

THE ISHMAELITE. I bought a prince for forty.

GAD. Then you shall have this prince for forty.

THE ISHMAELITE. Show him to me.

GAD. *(To Dan.)* Fish him out. *(Calls into the well.)* How is it with you now, Joseph? Here's a real rope. We're going to haul you out.

JOSEPH. Thank you, my brothers.

GAD. Careful. Hold tight. Don't fall and hurt yourself. *(Several of the brothers pull at the rope and haul Joseph out.)*

JOSEPH. *(Scrambles over the rim of the well.)* Jehovah has heard my prayers!

GAD. Why shouldn't He? Aren't you His favorite son?

JOSEPH. I knew He would not let me remain in that pit. *(The brothers turn Joseph so that his back is to the Ishmaelite and brush him off solicitously. They put on the coat of many colors and adjust it carefully. Gad spins Joseph about and exhibits him to the Ishmaelite.)*

GAD. Look him over. You will find him sound in flesh and wind.

JOSEPH. *(Drawing back.)* Who is this man?

DAN. Your new master.

JOSEPH. *(Suddenly changes his bearing and tone of voice. Ingratiatingly, to the Ishmaelite.)* How much are they trying to sell me for?

THE ISHMAELITE. Forty pieces of silver.

JOSEPH. They rob you. I'm just a bag of bones and soft

43

white meat. Softer than a chicken. Feel these muscles. I'm no good for anything.

THE ISHMAELITE. Don't overdo it. I really don't want to buy you.

GAD. Listen, slave-driver, he's a valuable article. (*Takes the coat off Joseph's shoulders and hands it to the Ishmaelite, who feels it expertly.*) Have you ever seen such a fine coat on an ordinary person? Doesn't that prove he's valuable?

THE ISHMAELITE. Since you put it that way, with the coat as part of the bargain—

DAN. (*Grabbing the coat out of the Ishmaelite's hands.*) What! The coat with him! Certainly not. What do you take us for?

THE ISHMAELITE. What value's he got without the coat? The deal is off. (*Starts off. Two brothers bring him back again.*)

GAD. All right—all right—he's yours for thirty pieces. But without the coat.

JOSEPH. One day's work out in the fields would kill me. And then where's your investment?

GAD. Let's settle it. He's yours for twenty. But twenty is bottom.

JOSEPH. (*As the Ishmaelite feels Joseph's arms and shoulders.*) Soft as chicken. I'm simply not worth buying.

THE ISHMAELITE. (*Takes a small wooden instrument from his pocket, pries open Joseph's mouth and examines it.*) I'll take him. My weakness—buying up odds and ends because they're bargains. (*Tosses a bag of coins into Zebulun's hands.*)

44

JOSEPH. Brothers, why do you hate me so?

GAD. If a man must have dreams, let him keep them to himself where they can harm no one.

THE ISHMAELITE. *(Matter-of-factly fastens shackles on Joseph's wrists. The shackles have a cord attached and he begins to lead Joseph off.)* Come along, valuable article. Let's travel now.

JOSEPH. *(Pulls away from him and runs over to his brothers.)* In Jehovah's name, don't sell me into slavery.

THE ISHMAELITE. *(Reaches Joseph and matter-of-factly cuts him sharply across the back with his whip.)* No, no —none of that!

JOSEPH. If you touch me again, I'll kill you.

THE ISHMAELITE. *(Calmly.)* Step along. *(As they move off to the sound of the whip.)* Being a slave's not such a bad life—once you get used to it.

JOSEPH. May the curse of Jehovah fall on you—and on my brothers. *(He and the Ishmaelite move off. Reuben is released. There is a long silence. Zebulun gives the silver to Gad.)*

REUBEN. *(Yanks the coat out of Dan's hands and holds it out.)* What have we done, brothers? We've sold our own flesh.

GAD. I didn't sell him for the money. *(Flings the bag of coins into the well.)* Now we are free of his wild dreams. *(The lights dim down very quickly, to be replaced by a deep blue-green light. In this light all the brothers, except Reuben, move off taking with them whatever hand props have to be removed from the stage.)*

Scene 2

*With no pause in the action, a spotlight picks up Reuben
as the Narrator. He moves to the side of the stage with
the coat of many colors in his hands and speaks directly
to the audience.*

REUBEN. We sprinkled the coat of many colors with
blood—blood taken from that three-month-old lamb which
Asher had killed. We brought the coat back to Jacob, the
father, and told him that some wild beast had devoured
Joseph. The father tore his clothes and wore sackcloth.
He would not be consoled. His tears washed the coat of
many colors.

As for Joseph, soon after the caravan reached Egypt, the
Ishmaelite sold him. In fact, Joseph was sold many, many,
many times. He was an irritating slave—comparing, criti-
cizing, suggesting changes in such a way as to make his
masters seem a bit stupid. Joseph was sold—and resold—
and sold again—and yet again, just to get rid of him. The
number of beatings he received is beyond counting—but he
would not learn that there was a direct connection between his tongue and his back—that whenever he opened

his mouth to criticize in that superior way of his, the inevitable result was a beating.

About three years after my brothers and I sold him to the Ishmaelite, he was sold into the house of Potiphar, chief advisor to Pharaoh. Again, because of an argument with an overseer, he was thrown into a dungeon and chained to that post. *(Joseph enters quietly and chains himself to the post. He slumps down in a position of exhaustion. The light on Reuben dims quickly to blackness. He moves off the stage as meanwhile, the deep blue-green light is replaced by the lighting required. The scene is a dungeon with a suggestion of bare walls of stone. The light is dim. There is one small grating high in a corner. The light sifting through the grating indicates that the place is underground.)*

JOSEPH. *(Getting to his knees.)* Hear me, Jehovah, hear my prayers. Help me out of this pit. By count of the light and dark coming through this grate, I have been cast down into this pit for seven days and seven nights. Enough, Jehovah. Please help me out of here. *(There is a silence.)* It is not entirely my fault that I am here. A good part of it—I am not saying how much—is Your fault, too. Please, don't get angry with me. Facts are facts, Jehovah, and the fact is that You gave me the brain I have and You surely gave it to me to use. It's this brain of mine, the one *You* gave me, that's getting me into trouble. *(Grudgingly.)* Maybe I *do* have a way of irritating people when I suggest a few dozen improvements. *(His voice rises to an angry roar as he gets to his feet, his chains rattling.)* Maybe I am impatient and let my temper get out of hand when I see so much stupidity all around me and when the stupid

47

men who rule me don't let me change things. *(Returns to his knees, speaks very gently.)* But I have learned my lesson, Jehovah. I'm going to be—*(With increasing contempt.)*—more cautious, more skillful, more diplomatic, more artful, more wily, more cunning, more beguiling, more devious. I promise it. Now it's up to You, Jehovah. Get me out of this pit. *(Silence for a moment.)* Jehovah! I'm calling on You. *(Silence.)* Jehovah! *(Silence.)* You cannot mean to abandon me. *(Silence.)* This pit is a grave. I have been dead long enough. Resurrect me. *(Silence for a moment. A heavy bolt is drawn. A door opens and a flood of sunlight streams down a crude staircase. Music is heard; it is music of the outside world, bustling and gay. A man and woman pause at the top, limned against the light. They are Vashnee, Potiphar's wife, and Arraffi, Chamberlain to Potiphar.*

Arraffi has dignity, wit and strength, which is combined with an ironic sobriety. Vashnee is a woman of wisdom and knowledge, an experienced courtier. She has an inner regality, and perhaps a rigidity, that indicates her disappointment with the sort of life which gives her no opportunity to use her talents directly.

They descend a few steps and stop on a landing. Joseph is alert and wary. He listens intently, meanwhile keeping himself concealed.)

VASHNEE. And this place? I never knew it existed. *(She goes down a few steps, then goes back to the landing.)* Aaigh! What a smell. Like a slimy pit.

ARRAFFI. Why must you go poking about all day? Up and down and around. I am tired. Why are you not content to walk in scented garden paths?

VASHNEE. Am I not mistress of this household?

ARRAFFI. Forgive me, my lady. The gods do strange things to men. I am sorry they made me a fool.

VASHNEE. I have offended you, Arraffi. Every time you take offense at me, you retreat into your maneuver of fool and foolery. The man charged with the care of the richest house in Egypt can scarcely be as great a fool as you now pretend to be.

ARRAFFI. *(With a touch of bitterness and self-irony.)* The gods do strange things to men who live by maneuver —who must always work through others and never receive credit or blame for the product of their ideas.

VASHNEE. *(Challenging him.)* But, Arraffi, don't you get any pleasure out of being the secret ruler of Egypt?

ARRAFFI. *(Stonily.)* Pharaoh, anointed of Isis, is ruler of Egypt.

VASHNEE. And who rules Pharaoh?

ARRAFFI. Every child knows that your husband, Potiphar, is chief advisor to Pharaoh.

VASHNEE. And who advises Potiphar how to advise Pharaoh?

ARRAFFI. I shall let you share a secret. Some of the best ideas I have given to your husband, who in turn gives them to Pharaoh as his own—some of these best ideas have come from you.

VASHNEE. *(Bows her head in acknowledgment.)* Are you never tempted to laugh when Potiphar takes your ideas and gives them to Pharaoh as his own?

ARRAFFI. And you? Are you never tempted to laugh

when I take your ideas and give them to your husband, Potiphar, as my own?

VASHNEE. My joke is too sad.

ARRAFFI. So is mine. . . . Come, let us go.

VASHNEE. I must go down into the dungeon, Arraffi.

ARRAFFI. Why, my lady?

VASHNEE. I am searching for something—and I do not know what it is.

ARRAFFI. This is hardly the place to pose me a riddle.

VASHNEE. For seven nights in succession I have dreamed this dream. I am to search for something until I find it. But the dream does not tell me what it is that I must find.

ARRAFFI. And what would you find here?

VASHNEE. Help me down these steps.

ARRAFFI. I have been up and down all the stairs I intend to climb today. I mean no disrespect for your dreams, my lady, nor for your ideas which I admire and have used, but they always end up in more work for me.

VASHNEE. How else can I do it? Just as you must work through other men, so must I work through you.

ARRAFFI. I have long thought of going into the desert, living there, contemplating the stars. I am tired of working through other men. I am tired of other men working me through. I have been tired of it for years. I have earned my rest. I am going within the month. I will tell Potiphar about it this very day.

VASHNEE. You can say, "I am old and tired," and go off into the desert. But I cannot say I am tired of my life and change it. I would still be wife to Potiphar. How will I manage if you go into the desert?

ARRAFFI. You will find a way, my lady. You always have. . . . Your present restlessness is too much for me. And this latest idea of yours these granaries to be built throughout the country.

VASHNEE. *(With a hint of irritation.)* I'm not asking you to build the granaries yourself, block by block.

ARRAFFI. I know. I know. You've already told it to me a hundred times.

VASHNEE. And I will tell it to you again and again until the urgency of what I am saying takes root.

ARRAFFI. I am going into the desert. I am going within the month. I will speak to Potiphar about it today.

VASHNEE. And who will replace you as Chamberlain?

ARRAFFI. Let Malfi have the job. He wants it badly enough.

VASHNEE. That fool. That ineffectual ninth son of a petty nobleman. Have mercy. Egypt would soon be in ruins with Malfi in charge.

ARRAFFI. Please—no appeals to my patriotism. It won't work. I once thought that I could not take time to die and go peacefully into my tomb until I found for Egypt a new burden-bearer. But I no longer believe I am indispensable. Egypt will survive—even with Malfi replacing me. . . . Come, let us go into the light. *(Vashnee reluctantly joins Arraffi. They move up a step or two. Joseph deliberately sighs heavily, half groaning, in order to attract*

51

their attention. Arraffi and Vashnee are startled and listen intently. They speak in low voices.)

VASHNEE. Did you hear something? Are there mice here?

ARRAFFI. No, my lady—only rats.

VASHNEE. *(Joseph groans deliberately.)* Are you sure rats are the only inhabitants?

ARRAFFI. Occasionally our overseers throw a lazy slave in here to reform him.

VASHNEE. But only last week you told me that we had no lazy slaves.

ARRAFFI. Ask me again tomorrow and I will tell you the same.

VASHNEE. What the gods have decreed cannot be changed.

ARRAFFI. The gods may have been kinder than you suspect. This cannot be so pleasant a place to spend one's days. Now fate has decreed an expeditious way for him to leave this dungeon.

VASHNEE. You mean at the hands of your ——? *(Makes a sign of a knife cutting a throat.)*

ARRAFFI. Physician. Exactly. *(Joseph groans again, deliberately.)*

VASHNEE. Poor wretch. Perhaps the gods *were* kind. May I speak to him, Arraffi, before you ——? *(Again makes sign of a knife cutting a throat.)*

ARRAFFI. Talk to him if you like. But my conversation will be more to the point. *(They go down the steps and come close to Joseph.)*

VASHNEE. What sort of slave are you?

JOSEPH. *(There is no self-pity. He is shrewd, possessed and maneuvering.)* One about to die.

ARRAFFI. The lady wishes to know if you are a prisoner taken in war or an ordinary slave.

JOSEPH. I am a bad slave and therefore as good as a dead slave.

ARRAFFI. I can see that you lack respect for your betters.

JOSEPH. Nothing will come of it—not even a beating. No one troubles to beat a dead dog.

ARRAFFI. *(To Vashnee.)* I'm sure you now understand why he has been thrown into solitary confinement. I have an excellent cure for that cough. I will go fetch the physician.

VASHNEE. *(In a softened tone.)* Is the matter so urgent?

ARRAFFI. The very essence of the art of healing lies in attacking the disease in time.

VASHNEE. Very well, Arraffi, bring your cure. I will stay and talk with him until you return.

ARRAFFI. Do you think that wise?

VASHNEE. Am I never to do anything except what is wise?

ARRAFFI. My lady has the power to do whatever she wishes. *(With his dagger he scratches a line on the wall opposite the open door.)* But when the sun travels to this mark I will return with my most expert surgeon. *(He starts off.)*

53

JOSEPH. Go. Get your executioner. And don't wait until the lines touch. Come back with him as quickly as you can.

ARRAFFI. I will not come back more quickly than I intended. You shall have your time. It is little enough. *(He goes.)*

VASHNEE. Do you know who I am?

JOSEPH. You're a fine lady bored with life who came down to this tomb in search of a sensation.

VASHNEE. Suppose I told you that I am your mistress, Vashnee, wife to Potiphar?

JOSEPH. When the worms get you, you'll not taste any the sweeter.

VASHNEE. I've a great mind to leave you to your fate.

JOSEPH. In three score years our fate will be the same. You could not change it if you tried.

VASHNEE. You are impertinent. *(Starts for the steps.)*

JOSEPH. *(Calling after her.)* And you are stupid.

VASHNEE. *(Stops, turns and moves toward him, her interest and curiosity heightened. Joseph is relieved that she has not gone.)* Why are you so insolent?

JOSEPH. *(With disarming candor.)* How else can I attract—and hold—your attention?

VASHNEE. *(With admiration.)* Who are you?

JOSEPH. *(With a suggestion of rattling his chains.)* A slave.

VASHNEE. You are no ordinary slave. What is your name?

JOSEPH. Joseph.

VASHNEE. Why were you sent here?

JOSEPH. A stupid overseer had me whipped and thrown in here because I told him how to farm to make the crop more plentiful. He blazed with anger, called the guard and cried, "Beat the Hebrew—beat the hide off him!" And as I was being lashed I heard him shout, "I farm as my father and grandfather before me." Fool! Ha!

VASHNEE. (Does not disbelieve him; she is testing him.) But you are young and our overseers are experienced farmers.

JOSEPH. I knew more about farming when I was ten than that fool will ever know. (Vashnee laughs.) You don't believe that my way was good.

VASHNEE. Why should I believe it?

JOSEPH. In Canaan, where I was reared, the land is arid. We had to learn many things to wrest our bread from it.

VASHNEE. But surely our overseers know more than a stray Hebrew.

JOSEPH. Egypt's poorest land is Canaan's best, yet we always raised plenty. You have so much water in Egypt. The sight of all this water drives me to a frenzy. I want to do something with it. And you get almost no benefit out of it. Oh, if I had the power to control the waters of Egypt! If your planters used our methods in this fertile soil, Egypt would be the richest country in the world.

VASHNEE. She is that now.

JOSEPH. I say Egypt is a poor nation.

VASHNEE. What can you, a mere slave, know of Egypt?

JOSEPH. More than you, a mere lady. I have been driven up and down this land. I know every corner of it.

VASHNEE. Then you must know that our harvest this year is more plentiful than usual.

JOSEPH. I know that Egypt lies like a fat cow in rich pasture—lazy and brainless, with no thought for the hard years which always follow the rich. And like that cow, she is marked for slaughter.

VASHNEE. You utter dire predictions with such an air of confidence. I can see why that overseer wanted to get rid of you.

JOSEPH. I hate stupid men! I hate them doubly when they have power over me. Every time I see one in authority, my muscles ache to get at his throat. How can Potiphar put up with such incompetence when even a minimum use of the human brain would double his riches! I could treble his riches.

VASHNEE. Being a slave has not killed your imagination.

JOSEPH. It is not imagination. It is brains.

VASHNEE. Your brains did not prevent you from becoming a slave. How do you explain that?

JOSEPH. My brothers hated me and sold me into Egypt. I had dreams that made them unhappy—that made them fear me. (*Challenging her.*) This miserable slave that you see, dreamt that they would all bow before him—that he would rule men and govern the greatest nation in the world.

VASHNEE. And what do you say of your dreams now?

56

Scene 2

JOSEPH. I say that I shall be ruler of Egypt. *(As Vashnee looks at the wall with its dagger mark.)* Ah, I know what you're thinking. You think when those two lines meet, the old man will come back with his executioner who will stick his dagger under my ribs—and then where are my dreams? *(Points to the wall and indicates the distance between the two lines with his thumb and forefinger.)* I have only this much time to convince you that I am the answer to your dreams and to that old man's need for a successor. *(Vashnee laughs with admiration.)* An hour ago, I was face to face with death, and yet—though I didn't know how He would do it, I knew that the hand of Jehovah—

VASHNEE. Who?

JOSEPH. Jehovah. The God of the Hebrews. My God . . . . I knew that the hand of Jehovah would pluck me out of this tomb, which is a pit.

VASHNEE. Has He? I don't notice you safely out of this pit.

JOSEPH. You will release me. You are the instrument of Jehovah. He made you descend into this pit to lift me up—for Jehovah intends to carry out His mighty plans through me. When I replace Arraffi and become the secret ruler of Egypt, then Egypt will have not only the services of a most able administrator, but she will have Jehovah thrown into the balance as well. *(Points.)* The line of the dagger and the line of the sun are nearly joined. The old man will be back in a moment. The fate of Egypt is in your hands.

VASHNEE. Your fate also rests in my hands.

JOSEPH. That too. But fix your attention on Egypt— not on me.

VASHNEE. *(With sharp change of manner. Urgently.)* You are right. Egypt does lie like a fat cow, lazy and brainless. Our surplus harvest is going to waste.

JOSEPH. Aha!

VASHNEE. I have a plan to save the surplus. If I persuade Arraffi to set you free, will you start working on my plan? I will help you.

JOSEPH. That depends on what your plan is. I, too, have plans for Egypt.

VASHNEE. You aren't even out of your chains, yet you presume to bargain with me.

JOSEPH. We need each other, my lady Vashnee. Why shouldn't I bargain with you? What is your plan?

VASHNEE. To set up granaries all over Egypt. Let it be proscribed by law that all surplus grain must be deposited in these granaries to be used when Egypt falls on lean years.

JOSEPH. Very good. Very good.

VASHNEE. If I maneuver it so that you will succeed Arraffi as Chamberlain to the house of my husband, Potiphar, do you swear to me a most holy oath by your Hebrew god that you will bend your energies toward the execution of this plan? *(Joseph is silent.)* Swear it, Joseph, swear it by your Hebrew god. I will help you. I can teach you.

JOSEPH. I admire your plan, my lady Vashnee, admire it very much indeed—save the grain of the years of plenty to tide over during the lean years. But I ask you to think for a moment—why are there fruitful years and why years of famine? Is there not a way to prevent the lean years?

58

VASHNEE. *(Sharply.)* Is there?

JOSEPH. There is. If we could control the water supply of the Nile by building dams—

VASHNEE. *(Cuts him off.)* The waters of Egypt, the rise and fall of the Nile, are in the hands of the sacred priesthood. That is the established order of life in Egypt.

JOSEPH. I have lived in Egypt long enough to know it.

VASHNEE. Your idea of controlling the water supply is very interesting—but impractical. It would cause too many changes.

JOSEPH. More than changes. It would transform Egypt —and for the better.

VASHNEE. No. It would throw Egypt into confusion. My plan, however—

JOSEPH. Your plan would merely soften the cycle of hunger. My dams would eliminate hunger.

VASHNEE. My granaries will take care of the immediate problem and they will strengthen the power of the Pharaoh. There could be no open opposition to such a plan— only approval and good wishes. *(Joseph makes as if to speak. Vashnee cuts him off. Arraffi appears at the stairs, followed by an executioner carrying an axe.)* Which is it to be? My plan or his executioner? *(There is a pause.)* I am firm on these conditions, Joseph.

JOSEPH. I accept your terms.

VASHNEE. Arraffi, I have found him! I have your successor for you!

ARRAFFI. *(Descends the stairs. The executioner remains at the head of the stairs.)* That thing. . . . Come here, my successor, I cannot see you.

Act I

JOSEPH. I am chained. You must come to me.

VASHNEE. He is shrewd, wise, bold and daring. He has courage—and a sense of destiny.

ARRAFFI. (Stands before Joseph, mocking.) Shrewd, wise, bold and daring. Courage. A sense of destiny. (Laughs.)

VASHNEE. Try him. Try him. Within a month your opinion of him will change. (Arraffi stands before Joseph, studying him in silent indecision.)

JOSEPH. Make up your mind, old man. Are you always so slow? Decide and act.

ARRAFFI. Hold your tongue. You are gambling with your life.

JOSEPH. I would have been dead long before this were I afraid to gamble. Unfasten my chains, old man. I have work to do. (Music of the outside world is heard, joyous and strong.) I belong to life! (Arraffi moves to Joseph and takes the lock in his hand. The lights dim down very quickly, to be replaced by the deep blue-green light. In this light, Joseph, Arraffi, Vashnee and the executioner move off the stage.)

Scene 3

There is no pause in the action. A spotlight picks up Reuben, the Narrator, as he comes to the front of the stage. He is playing an Egyptian flute. He stops and speaks to the audience.

REUBEN. Vashnee was right. Within a month, Arraffi had changed his opinion of Joseph. Within two months, he knew he had found his successor. Before the year was over, Arraffi retired in favor of Joseph and went off into the desert for rest and contemplation. And Joseph, the new Chamberlain, took over the complete management of the house of Potiphar, becoming, as Arraffi before him, the secret ruler of Egypt. *(Potiphar, Vashnee, Asenath and Malfi enter and take their places. Asenath wears a garland of bells in her hair which tinkle gaily as she moves about. The deep blue-green light is replaced by the lighting required for this scene.)* In this household there is Potiphar, Governor of Egypt, Vashnee and their twelve-year old daughter, Princess Asenath. There is also Malfi, who is now Joseph's assistant. He was assistant to Arraffi and expected to succeed him. But Joseph came along and Malfi

61

remained where he was—assistant. He seems doomed to remain the eternal assistant.

(It is three years later.

A room in Potiphar's palace. It is simply furnished; a few gilded stools, Joseph's desk and chair, the fishing tank. On the right, an opening looking out on a public place; on the left, an opening on a private garden.

Potiphar is seated on a stool. In common with many of the Egyptian nobility, he is fishing out of a glorified fishing tank. His fishing pole is a short, black, intricately carved wand, generously studded with jewels. The golden collar and official outer robe of the Governor of Egypt are placed by his side. Potiphar is cynical and indolent, but he is no fool. He knows how to take advantage of the moment and he understands the art of choosing excellent administrators and of using their brains.

Malfi, Second Chamberlain to Potiphar, stands beside him with a papyrus partly unrolled in his hands. Malfi is about thirty years old. He seems a willful man and a dangerous opponent, though he is not over-clever. Envy is his guiding passion.

Vashnee and Princess Asenath are seated at Joseph's desk. Asenath is doing a small drawing as Vashnee looks on.

Potiphar, Vashnee, Asenath and Malfi continue in pantomime as Reuben says.)

REUBEN. Potiphar is indulging in the Egyptian custom of indoor fishing. He is acknowledged by all as one of the most skillful in Egypt; medals, trophies, awards. He has an entire wall mounted with mummified specimens, proof of his prowess, amongst which are to be seen some of the most exquisite miniatures in all of Egypt. He holds the

Egyptian record for the smallest fish caught on a hook.
The fish he is working on now are a new breed of fighters
which Vashnee, a most capable wife, imported at great ex-
pense from Ethiopia. . . . And here, seated at Joseph's desk,
are Vashnee and Princess Asenath. . . . Oh, yes. That's
Malfi, Joseph's assistant. . . . Potiphar likes appropriate
music when he fishes. *(He goes to the side and begins playing softly. It is the Potiphar theme. The action of the
scene proceeds.)*

MALFI. *(Refers to his papyrus.)* This is the last item,
Potiphar. A Phoenician ship loaded with spices and slaves—

POTIPHAR. *(Fishing intently.)* Sssshhhh! *(Malfi forgets
about the business at hand. Potiphar and he concentrate
on the fishing. Potiphar almost hooks a fish, but does not
make the strike.)*

MALFI. *(Trying again.)* A Phoenician ship loaded with—

POTIPHAR. *(Crossly to Reuben.)* Is it your intention to
put the fish to sleep? Let the music be wilder. Agitate the
fish. I want action. These are Ethiopian fighters. *(Reuben
plays. It is the Potiphar theme but played wildly.)*

MALFI. *(Shouting to be heard above the music.)* This
ship loaded with spices and slaves rounded the bend before sunrise— *(Breaking off and watching the fishing intently.)* There he goes! *(He leans over.)*

POTIPHAR. You're casting a shadow!

MALFI. *(Drawing back hastily.)* Excuse me.

POTIPHAR. *(Irritated.)* This is the third time this month.
It's becoming serious.

MALFI. I am sorry, Potiphar. I'll be more careful.

POTIPHAR. *(Waves impatiently at Reuben.)* Let there be silence. Maybe a change of pace will work. *(Reuben stops playing. To Malfi.)* And you, Malfi. I don't want to be bothered with these problems. The annual fishing tournament is less than a month off and I need practice. Joseph is First Chamberlain. Joseph handles these matters. Go ask Joseph.

MALFI. I brought this to your attention only because Joseph is so busy with his plans for the building of the granaries.

POTIPHAR. Sssshhhh. *(The fishing proceeds in silence. Asenath shows Vashnee the drawing.)*

VASHNEE. No. No. No. Let me show you. *(She works on the drawing with Asenath watching studiously.)* And, furthermore, you should know by now that no emotion is to be shown when drawing the face of an Egyptian. You can show emotion on the face of a slave, on the face of a foreigner, on the face of a prisoner captured in war. But when you draw the face of an Egyptian, it is to be serene, with no trace of emotion whatsoever.

ASENATH. If I were to draw the face of Joseph, would it be with or without emotion?

VASHNEE. Of course without emotion.

ASENATH. But, mother, he is a foreigner, and you yourself have told me that he is a bought slave.

VASHNEE. You do have a way of raising the most difficult—*(Breaks off.)* Please, a bit of quiet while I concentrate on what I'm doing.

MALFI. *(Begins once more.)* This is the last item. A Phoenician ship loaded with spices and slaves rounded the bend before sunrise this morning. Our runners saw the flaming red sails—

POTIPHAR. *(Absent-mindedly.)* Slaves did you say—spices and slaves?

MALFI. Yes. Strong young slaves *(As Potiphar is about to make a strike.)* There he goes. A little to the left. He's close. You're getting it.

POTIPHAR. *(Misses the strike and utters a snort of disgust.)* Aaaagh! *(Joseph enters. Asenath moves away from Vashnee, who continues drawing, and shyly goes to one side. She stares at Joseph.)*

JOSEPH. *(To Potiphar.)* Any luck?

POTIPHAR. Not a thing. They're just not biting today. Tried everything—hooks, lures, feathers, flies.

JOSEPH. *(To Malfi, who has hastily rolled up the papyrus and is shoving it in the fold of his robe.)* Trying to go over my head again? You should know better than that by now. Out with it. What's the business?

MALFI. I was only telling Potiphar that a Phoenician ship rounded the bend before sunrise this morning. They have spices and strong young slaves from the Aramaic wars. *(To Potiphar)* Let's buy a hundred slaves in total and I'll buy in my usual ten percent.

JOSEPH. Not from the Aramaic wars, but from the Sumerian wars. And we get no spices from the Phoenicians, only purple dyes.

MALFI. I bow. *(To Potiphar.)* Is it Potiphar's pleasure that we buy these admirable slaves for his new estate?

65

POTIPHAR. Must I tell you again not to annoy me with such details! That's Joseph's business.

MALFI. It shall not occur again. *(To Joseph, with ill-concealed venom.)* The ears of Potiphar's Second Chamberlain are now ready to receive the words of wisdom from the lips of Potiphar's First Chamberlain.*(Music and the noise of a holiday crowd are heard from outside. Reuben answers the music on his flute in a sort of obbligato.)*

ASENATH. *(Joyfully.)* The feast in honor of the God Ptah! *(Runs to Potiphar and shakes his fishing wand impatiently.)* Father, take me to the feast.

POTIPHAR. I'm sorry, but I have to disappoint you.

ASENATH. Oh, father.

POTIPHAR. I haven't had a strike all morning. *(To Reuben.)* Play. Softly. Maybe we can seduce them to the hook. *(Reuben plays softly.)*

MALFI. *(To Asenath.)* Perhaps Joseph will take you. One of our poor Egyptian religious celebrations would amuse him after his elaborate and ceremonial tribal holidays.

ASENATH. *(Turning to Joseph, shyly.)* Will you take me, Joseph?

JOSEPH. Malfi is teasing you. He knows that I never attend your religious festivals.

ASENATH. Don't you like them? I think they're very gay.

JOSEPH. I'm sure they are. But I have work to do.

ASENATH. Why can't you stop work for one single morning? Why can't you? One single, little morning, Joseph? *(She dances and pirouettes about half-shyly, half-teasingly. The bells in her hair tinkle merrily.)*

VASHNEE. *(Quietly to Joseph, so that the others don't hear.)* Go, Joseph, take her to the feast. She adores you.

JOSEPH. Her enthusiastic outbursts, her excesses, her almost irrational exuberance—I don't know how to cope with her.

VASHNEE. Asenath is still a child, but give her three years. The bud will bloom. Her beauty will surpass mine. *(Joseph makes a deprecating gesture.)* Take her to the feast. It means so much to her.

JOSEPH. *(To Asenath.)* Asenath, stop prancing. Come here. *(She does.)* I will take you to your feast.

ASENATH. What a lovely, thoughtful, kind, generous, wonderful man you are. *(Impulsively, she takes his hand and kisses it. Joseph draws it away, embarrassed.)* Can we go this minute, this very minute?

JOSEPH. I have about an hour of work. Come back then and we'll go.

ASENATH. How happy, how happy I am.

VASHNEE. *(To Asenath, who is dancing off.)* I'll join you in a few minutes. I think I'll teach you how to make up your eyes. You're just about old enough. *(Asenath goes. At an inconspicuous moment during the following, Reuben leaves the stage.)*

JOSEPH. *(Incisively to Malfi.)* About those slaves. Be at the landing when the ship docks. Praise their quality and strength.

MALFI. Are we buying or selling?

67

JOSEPH. Enhance their value in the Phoenicians' eyes so that they will raise the price for them. Then get a price of the entire cargo, slaves and dyes together.

MALFI. And give them a shipload of gold in exchange, I suppose.

JOSEPH. No doubt they will ask that, being traders. When they do, deduct the price of the slaves from the price of the entire cargo and buy the dye stuffs only at the low rate.

MALFI. Don't you want the slaves?

JOSEPH. Slaves can be bought anywhere; only Phoenicians have purple dyes. *(Potiphar chuckles admiringly.)*

MALFI. *(Bows to Joseph.)* Again, I bow! But tell me, Joseph, have you no fear that after you have taught me all your Hebrew tricks, I may supplant you as Potiphar's First Chamberlain?

JOSEPH. If I should die suddenly you might supplant me, Malfi. *(Malfi, startled, looks at Joseph. Joseph meets his gaze with a mask-like expression.)* But since you are older than I, which of us do you think will die first?

MALFI. Who can tell when the gods may decree a death?

POTIPHAR. True—very true, Joseph. Sometimes at night when I remember that you are an infidel and a heathen, I am troubled for fear some evil may touch you. You know, you can't expect the gods to watch over you as carefully as they do over Malfi, Vashnee, Asenath and me.

MALFI. Potiphar is right, as always. It is very wrong of you to tempt the gods by unbelief. I tremble to think what might happen if they should suddenly decree that I, the

Second Chamberlain and a mere Egyptian, had to carry on the great work of the Hebrew foreigner.

JOSEPH. *(Smiles ironically.)* Have you never heard of the great God, Jehovah, who has a special preference for Hebrews? I am told that He even prefers them to Egyptians.

POTIPHAR. How can you jest so about sacred things, Joseph? You know that the gods of Egypt are the only true gods.

JOSEPH. *(To Malfi.)* Well, in any event, I have one consolation for you. When you die and appear before the throne of Osiris, that great god may make you his First Chamberlain, since I won't be there to stand in your way. When I die, I go to the God, Jehovah.

POTIPHAR. Jehovah. Jehovah. A peculiar name.

JOSEPH. Not at all peculiar as a god, though. He has all the orthodox godly attributes—omniscience—omnipotence—omnipresence. And Jehovah, who is inscrutable, like Osiris, allows death to reach out and take the old and withered, or the young and beautiful, in haphazard fashion.

MALFI. *(His voice breaking, but there is an undertone of hypocrisy.)* My wife—my beautiful young wife. Did death have to strike her? Why couldn't the gods have chosen another woman?

VASHNEE. Their ways are not our ways. And it's not for us to question what they do.

MALFI. She was so beautiful!

VASHNEE. She *was* beautiful.

69

MALFI. I had her only a short time. She still loved me.

JOSEPH. She was very fond of figs, wasn't she? *(Malfi is startled.)* Just before she died, I was sitting here where we are now and she brought me a bowl of choice ones from your garden—with your compliments, I believe?

MALFI. Yes!

JOSEPH. I remember they were spiced in a new fashion with some rare seasoning that I had never seen used on figs before. The odor was delicious. But I was suffering from a fever and my physician had forbidden me to eat spiced fruits.

MALFI. But you allowed her to eat them!

JOSEPH. I insisted—especially when she told me you picked them with your own hands. They were such beautiful figs. And she had no fever—till after she had eaten them. *(Malfi draws his dagger and tries to stab Joseph. Joseph disarms him.)*

POTIPHAR. Was there something wrong with those figs, Joseph?

JOSEPH. Malfi seems to think so. *(Malfi, trembling, sinks to his knees and bows his head. Potiphar takes an ornamented sword and advances on Malfi. Malfi is between Joseph and Potiphar, terror-stricken. At appropriate times in the scene, he moans softly. Potiphar raises the sword. Vashnee stays Potiphar's hand, takes the sword from him and ceremoniously offers it to Joseph.)*

VASHNEE. Would you like the satisfaction of turning him into carrion, Joseph? It's your privilege, you know.

JOSEPH. *(Takes the sword and passes it back to Potiphar.)* Who would take his place as Second Chamberlain?

POTIPHAR. *(Shocked and annoyed, pressing the sword into Joseph's hand.)* This is no time to talk of that!

JOSEPH. *(Firmly refusing it.)* It's the only time, Potiphar. As usual, you are overlooking the practical aspect of the case.

POTIPHAR. I refuse to be practical until justice is done.

JOSEPH. It will be too late then.

POTIPHAR. *(To Malfi.)* Ingrate! You've gotten rich out of Joseph's brains. Is this the way you pay him back?

VASHNEE. *(Again takes the sword from Potiphar and puts it into Joseph's hands.)* The fellow tried to murder you. Can't I get that simple fact into your head?

JOSEPH. *(Again returns the sword to Potiphar.)* I know. I've known for ten days.

POTIPHAR. I hate to say this, Joseph, because I like you. But sometimes I wonder if you're really human. You don't seem to have any human feelings left at all. Why, I'd never think of letting the fellow live even one day after he tried to murder me. *(Vashnee takes the sword out of Potiphar's hands and presses it on Joseph.)*

JOSEPH. Why not—if you find him useful?

POTIPHAR. It's not right—it's not human.

JOSEPH. There's only one man in all Egypt who has it in his power to harm me. *(Takes sword out of Vashnee's hands and returns it to Potiphar.)*

POTIPHAR. Don't worry about the Pharaoh. He wouldn't hurt a flea if I told him it was my friend.

JOSEPH. It is not the Pharaoh who frightens this particular flea.

71

VASHNEE. Then who is it?

JOSEPH. Myself.

POTIPHAR. What! Now that's absurd. Why next to me, you're the most important man in Egypt.

JOSEPH. If anyone destroys me, it will be myself. *(Vashnee has taken the sword out of Potiphar's hands and presses it into Joseph's, who presses it back into Potiphar's hands.)*

POTIPHAR. What you need, Joseph, is a good physic. Tell me, do you eat plenty of fresh fruit and green vegetables?

JOSEPH. Yes—and I drink a jug of Nile water every morning as regularly as any fish.

POTIPHAR. Does it—are you all right that way?

JOSEPH. Perfect. I no longer need a sun dial to mark time. But in spite of that, I still think Malfi is worth more to us alive than dead.

POTIPHAR. Think of the danger! You can't afford to take such risks in your position.

JOSEPH. It will be easy to insure me against harm from Malfi. He tried to kill me because it was to his advantage to have me out of the way. Make it more to his advantage to have me alive, and he will be just as eager to protect me as he was to murder me.

POTIPHAR. If I were in the position of the gods, I'd be glad to arrange things that way, but I'm not.

JOSEPH. All you have to do is tell your soldiers throughout Egypt that on the day of my death—no matter what the cause—Malfi must also die in the same way.

72

MALFI. *(Raising his head but still on his knees, in protest.)* But, Joseph, this would mean that if you were bathing in the Nile, and a sacred crocodile swallowed you—I, too, would be thrown to the crocodiles. Is that fair? Is it just?

JOSEPH. No. But it's very convenient for me. I imagine that you will be very careful to see that no sacred crocodile dines in this fashion.

MALFI. I will do everything in my power. But such things are in the hands of the gods.

JOSEPH. Then you might pray occasionally for my safety—after you've done everything else you can in a practical way.

MALFI. I will. I promise you. I will pray for you night and day.

POTIPHAR. *(Laughs with huge enjoyment.)* It's beginning to work already! He's an entirely different man.

VASHNEE. He does seem to be more public spirited. But don't forget to issue the order to the police.

POTIPHAR. Have no fear. It shall be done before meat or drink passes my lips again.

VASHNEE. Good. And now that the house of Potiphar is once again in order, I shall join my daughter and teach her the art of beauty. *(She goes.)*

POTIPHAR. *(Chuckles.)* Marvelous, perfectly marvelous. Like that— *(Snaps his fingers.)* You change your worst enemy into your best friend. *(Puts the sword away and then puts on the golden collar and the official outer robe of the Governor of Egypt.)* I'm off to tell the Pharaoh. Hereafter I think we'll do this to all our political prisoners instead of chopping off their heads. *(Starts to go, then turns.)* What's the name of that god who looks after you Hebrews?

JOSEPH. Jehovah.

POTIPHAR. Jehovah. Well—He seems to have done pretty well by you, so far. But I still say that an important man like you shouldn't depend on a heathen god at a time like this. *(Leaves.)*

JOSEPH. *(As a blare of trumpets is heard.)* What is that infernal noise?

MALFI. Joseph, I must ask you to speak more respectfully of the gods of Egypt. Those are the trumpets in honor of the god, Ptah.

JOSEPH. That's no reason for you to stand around here all day. Get out and buy those dye stuffs.

MALFI. I'll do it immediately. *(Imploringly.)* And, Joseph, you *will* take care of yourself, won't you?

JOSEPH. *(Picks up the dagger and politely hands it to Malfi.)* No. That's your business now.

(Malfi hurries out. Joseph goes to the window and watches the holiday crowd outside with marked disapproval. Arraffi enters quietly in the garb of a desert hermit and stands looking at Joseph, who is not aware of his presence. A change has come over Arraffi. There is no longer any suggestion of the diplomat or politician about him. His eyes are understanding, though, at times, they have a cynical glitter in them. He shows a genial, amused affection for Joseph, who in turn gives him love and deference.)

ARRAFFI. I may as well go back to my desert.

74

JOSEPH. Arraffi! I'm glad to see you!

ARRAFFI. Are you sure? A moment ago you looked as cheerful as a mummy.

JOSEPH. I feel a little like one.

ARRAFFI. What's troubling you now?

JOSEPH. This stupid gaiety maddens me. Myriads of people moving to the one holiday spot, like sheep following a blind shepherd. Dancing. Singing.

ARRAFFI. Come, Joseph. You're annoyed because the priests have taken these dancers and singers away from you and your tasks for a day.

JOSEPH. To work, to change, to transform the world. That's the source of joy and excitement in a man's life. That giddy gaiety is not real joy!

ARRAFFI. Perhaps for them it is. All they know about your grand plans to transform the world is that it means more work for them. You don't know these people. Have you ever wondered what they're thinking about when they do your work? You may be in for a surprise if you ever find out. . . . Let them be gay and buzz like flies for their one day. They'll go back to work tomorrow. Your tasks will be finished in good time.

JOSEPH. I see that the desert agrees with you. What do you do there?

ARRAFFI. Things just as important as those I used to do here. On fine days I lie naked in the sand and watch the sun rise and set.

JOSEPH. And at night—you sleep?

75

ARRAFFI. Not always. Sometimes I count the stars.

JOSEPH. But you are at peace with the world and yourself. How wonderful to achieve such a state of grace.

ARRAFFI. To be rich in contemplation of the sun? Do you think that would ever satisfy you?

JOSEPH. No. I would have to possess it—harness it—command it to do my bidding.

ARRAFFI. *(Dryly.)* Then have it shine more temperately over my share of the desert during the burning noon hours.

JOSEPH. It shall be as you wish.

ARRAFFI. And above all, I beseech you, let the dawn and sunset always burst in glorious colors.

JOSEPH. I'll make a note of it.

ARRAFFI. You almost persuade me to believe you can.

JOSEPH. I must rule this earth as the sun rules the heavens, so that it may become a bright and glorious place where men no longer crawl in filth and poverty and ignorance, but walk as gods.

ARRAFFI. The sun and you!

JOSEPH. Yes. The sun and I! Arraffi, a fine new world where art, philosophy, science—all flourish under the guidance of one benevolent, intelligent ruler.

ARRAFFI. Rulers we have had with us always, but when have they ever been both benevolent and intelligent? Where shall we find this rare man?

JOSEPH. I am the man.

ARRAFFI. Naturally. . . . How are you not susceptible to the weakness and corruptibility of other men?

76

JOSEPH. I rule Egypt by Jehovah's will. The power invested in me is Jehovah's expression of His great design. I am the means through which He will achieve it.

ARRAFFI. Ah, Joseph, do not project your virtues to Jehovah. He doesn't need it. . . . An amazing man. You are not prepared to say, "I am a great man because I am a great man." But, rather you say, "I am a great man because Jehovah is with me." In short, you are prepared to take credit for everything but yourself. . . . Enough of that. I understand you have some bold and secret engineering project.

JOSEPH. Not so secret if a hermit out in the desert hears of it.

ARRAFFI. I am told about those things I wish to be told about. But this confuses me. It seems to be two projects, one modifying the other.

JOSEPH. Or, perhaps one masking the intention of the other?

ARRAFFI. So that's it.

JOSEPH. *(Unlocks a drawer of the desk and extracts several maps and charts.)* Potiphar knows that I am working on plans for a series of granaries and he thinks that is the extent of my work. But for nearly a year I've been working on these plans—plans which will—

ARRAFFI. Show them to me.

JOSEPH. If I could only bring these plans to the Pharaoh.

ARRAFFI. You will never see the Pharaoh. If Potiphar were to bring the Pharaoh and you together, what would happen to him? Within a month you would be made

Governor of Egypt. Your brains—your anonymous brains —are a tremendous asset to Potiphar. Would he be foolish enough to throw this asset away by bringing the Pharaoh and you together? . . . Show me the plans. The true ones, not the mask.

JOSEPH. *(Lays them out.)* I'm going to build a series of dams all along the Nile. I'm going to regulate the water supply—

ARRAFFI. Bereft. Utterly bereft of your senses. Dams along the Nile.

JOSEPH. *(Continues unruffled.)* The dams will insure a uniform water supply. Consequently, the crops—

ARRAFFI. *(Impatiently, with some bitterness.)* I know. I know. You think it never occurred to me? *(Joseph is amazed.)* I thought you'd become enough of an Egyptian to understand this. Do you want to lose your head? You push this thing too far and the priests will bury you for it.

JOSEPH. I will build my dams whether the priests like it or not.

ARRAFFI. The water belongs to the priests. They've made a miracle of it. Its coming and going, its ebb and flow—that's all sacred in Egypt. And sooner than let you touch it—

JOSEPH. Priests or no priests, I will give Egypt enough food so that she can live.

ARRAFFI. You against the priesthood.

JOSEPH. When the people of Egypt see what I have done for them, they will love me and come over to my side.

ARRAFFI. *(Attracted by singing in the courtyard. Looks out.)* Is that Vashnee out there?

JOSEPH. *(Joins him.)* Yes.

ARRAFFI. Ah! She's taken to dyeing her hair.

JOSEPH. Has she? I hadn't noticed.

ARRAFFI. And I suppose you hadn't noticed that she's wearing more—shall we say—"interesting" gowns these days.

JOSEPH. I have other things to occupy my mind

ARRAFFI. *(Studies Joseph intently.)* And you've no idea why she's taken to wearing these interesting gowns? *(Vashnee's voice, accompanied by a lyre, is heard singing the Vashnee theme.)* She's coming this way. I must go.

JOSEPH. Why are you so eager to avoid her?

ARRAFFI. You will know soon enough. Tell Vashnee your dreams. She will interpret them for you. *(Starts off, laughing gently.)*

JOSEPH. Where are you going?

ARRAFFI. To the high places of the temple first, then back to my desert.

JOSEPH. What will *you* do in the temple—you who believe in nothing?

ARRAFFI. I shall pray earnestly that you, my son, who knows nothing that is of any value, may acquire wisdom before it is too late. *(He goes quickly. A charming-looking young girl, playing the Vashnee theme on a lyre, enters, followed by Vashnee who makes a grand entrance. With a wave of her hand, Vashnee dismisses the lyrist, who goes. Vashnee has changed her clothes and is now wearing a beautiful and daring gown. Until indicated, Vashnee and Joseph engaged in artificial court banter meanwhile cautiously looking about.)*

79

VASHNEE. Why, Joseph, are you still here? I thought you went away with my husband.

JOSEPH. Potiphar is with the Pharaoh, whose sacred countenance I am not permitted to gaze upon. When will Potiphar take me to the Pharaoh?

VASHNEE. Potiphar was quite angry the last time you mentioned it.

JOSEPH. So—I shall never gaze upon the Pharaoh?

VASHNEE. *(Exhibits herself gaily.)* You may gaze upon my holiday gown instead. *(Drawing it tight so as to bring out her figure.)* I think it clings too much. What do you think?

JOSEPH. *(Bows and speaks with formal respect.)* I stand before the most beautiful and most gracious woman in all Egypt.

VASHNEE. I asked your opinion of my dress. It *must* cling if all you can see is the woman it's supposed to conceal.

JOSEPH. I assure you I have seen nothing I should not see.

VASHNEE. *(After another cautious look about, nods her head affimatively.)* No one. It is safe. *(They drop pretense and embrace, kissing passionately. They freeze while kissing and are motionless. The lights on this area dim somewhat, cross-fading to a spotlight which picks up Reuben, as the Narrator, who enters downstage with a large Bible in his hands.)*

REUBEN. *(Reading from the Bible.)* And it came to pass that his master's wife cast her eyes upon Joseph and she

80

said, "Lie with me." But he refused and said unto her, "Behold, there is none greater in this house than I. My master hath kept back nothing from me but thee, because thou art his wife. How then can I do this great wickedness?" And she spoke to Joseph, day by day, but he hearkened not unto her. And one day when Joseph was in the house, she caught him by his garment saying, "Lie with me." And he left his garment in her hand and fled. When her lord came home, she said, "The Hebrew servant came in to lie with me, but I cried out with a loud voice. And when he heard my voice, he left his garment with me and fled." When his master heard the words of his wife, his wrath was kindled. And he took Joseph and put him into the prison where the king's prisoners were bound. (*Looks at Joseph and Vashnee, then shakes his head with wry humor.*) I wish the author were more accurate. That's not the way it happened. It is true, of course, that Joseph was charged with rape and sent to prison for two years, but not for the reason ascribed in this book. (*He exits. The spotlight blacks out as the general lighting is restored. Joseph and Vashnee unfreeze.*)

JOSEPH. Will I lie with you tonight?

VASHNEE. Perhaps. It depends on how well the lesson goes.

JOSEPH. What lesson are you talking about?

VASHNEE. (*Takes up the plans which Joseph had placed on the desk.*) These are the plans for the granaries? (*Joseph nods affirmatively.*) And construction will begin in two or three months?

JOSEPH. About that time. Surely no more than six.

Act I

VASHNEE. *(Studying one of them.)* A pity I don't know how to read plans so that I wouldn't have to be bothering you.

JOSEPH. It's no bother, Vashnee. I enjoy it.

VASHNEE. Do you enjoy it? . . . For months you've been promising to teach me how to read plans. I would like you to start. Right now.

JOSEPH. Not today, Vashnee. Please. Another time.

VASHNEE. Today. Now. *(Joseph takes a plan, unrolls it and lays it on the desk. Vashnee rolls it up, puts it back, takes another from the desk and unrolls it.)* No. This one.

JOSEPH. Please, Vashnee. Let me do the—

VASHNEE. This one.

JOSEPH. Why?

VASHNEE. My mood.

JOSEPH. *(Firmly picks up the plan he selected. With equal firmness, Vashnee puts it aside in favor of hers. After a silence, Joseph says.)* This symbol represents the walls of a granary.

VASHNEE. Forgive my question—it stems from ignorance. Do you mean that this symbol represents the walls of a granary—or that it represents a wall in general?

JOSEPH. Yes.

VASHNEE. It could, to take a far-fetched example, represent the wall of a dam, couldn't it ——

JOSEPH. It could—if we were discussing dams. But we are talking about granaries.

VASHNEE. —— for there are only three walls, which makes sense if it were a dam, but not if it were a granary?

JOSEPH. A detail. The fourth wall hasn't been drawn in.

VASHNEE. I thought you had a better staff of engineers than that.

JOSEPH. *(Is acutely uncomfortable.)* These lines represent separate storage compartments in the granary.

VASHNEE. Again, you must forgive my lack of experience in this matter, but couldn't these lines signify not separate storage compartments for grain, but dividing walls for more efficient control of the water? Go on, Joseph. *(Joseph is silent.)* And surely these wavy lines could be symbols for flowing water. Is that not so, Joseph?

JOSEPH. Enough, Vashnee. What is the meaning of all this?

VASHNEE. But that is precisely the question I was going to ask you. Two sets of plans. One contradicting the other. What is the meaning of it?

JOSEPH. Vashnee, I wish you wouldn't bother your beautiful head about this.

VASHNEE. *(In cold fury.)* Don't you dare speak to me that way. *(She controls herself superbly and speaks calmly.)* What is the meaning of these two sets of plans? *(Joseph is silent.)* I demand an answer of you, Joseph.

JOSEPH. Demand?

VASHNEE. Demand. I warn you, Joseph, though I saved your life and made you virtual ruler here, don't try my patience too far.

JOSEPH. It is natural for you to believe that you saved

my life and placed me where I am. But you were only an instrument in the hands of my Hebrew God, Jehovah. Why this sudden talk about dams?

VASHNEE. I had a chat with one of your engineers. You may think you have a loyal staff, but the very first one I approached couldn't resist my offer.

JOSEPH. Who?

VASHNEE. An indiscreet question. . . . On one side, in payment for the information I wanted, a bag of gold. On the other, for his first week of silence, I would cut off his right hand to the wrist; for the second week of silence, his right arm to the elbow; for the third week of silence, his right arm to the shoulder. For the next three weeks of silence, his left arm would be treated in like fashion. For the seventh week of silence, since it would seem he had no need for his tongue, I would have it cut out. Faced with these alternatives, your very loyal engineer quickly gave me the information I sought.

JOSEPH. *(Quietly.)* I am going ahead with the building of the dams.

VASHNEE. Did you not in that dungeon swear to me by your Hebrew god, Jehovah, that you would work on my plan for the granaries?

JOSEPH. *(Primly.)* I did not swear by Jehovah. I would not take Jehovah's name in vain.

VASHNEE. Then what did you do?

JOSEPH. I was silent when you asked me to swear by Jehovah. I only promised. I did not swear.

VASHNEE. You cunning Hebrew. You have lied to me

for a year. . . . I order you, Joseph, to drop the project for the dams at once. It will fail.

JOSEPH. You cannot order me. I am more powerful than you.

VASHNEE. You have lost your sense of reality, Joseph. Very well, I will not order you—I *beg* you to drop the project. It will fail and in the process will wreck everything we have together built for Egypt.

JOSEPH. *(With a great cry.)* I cannot stop. I am driven to it. I must build the dams.

VASHNEE. I will find a way to immobilize you.

JOSEPH. That you cannot do, Vashnee. I am too strong. *(Vashnee takes off her outer blouse and gives it to Joseph. Joseph, alarmed and at a loss.)* What are you doing?

VASHNEE. At best your dams are for the far future; my granaries are for today. And the priesthood won't oppose my plan. It is for this reason, as a statesman that I must— *(Turns toward the window and shouts.)* Help! Help! Help!

JOSEPH. What are you doing?

VASHNEE. *(Suddenly embraces and kisses him passionately. Joseph struggles to pull away, but Vashnee holds on to him. It is a comic moment.)* You are an extraordinary man. It grieves me to do this but it is necessary — *(Vashnee's hands move to the clasp holding Joseph's outer garment. She unloosens the clasp and then, disengaging herself from his embrace, gives his garment a sharp pull. It comes off in her hands. Joseph is dressed in nothing but a loin cloth and sandals.)*

85

Act I

JOSEPH. *(Advancing on her.)* Give me back my robe. *(Vashnee dances away from him.)* Vashnee, I warn you. You were the instrument of Jehovah when you took me out of that dungeon.

VASHNEE. If I was the instrument of Jehovah when I took you out of that dungeon, then equally, I am the instrument of Jehovah now. *(Rapidly divests herself of another garment and throws it at him. She is now clothed only in her scanty undergarments.)* Here. *(Joseph reaches out automatically and catches it with his free hand. He has one of her outer garments in each of his hands.)* It is He who is causing me to go to this window and shout— *(Goes to window and calls out in a great voice.)* Rape! Rape! Help! Rape! Help! Rape! Help! *(Back to Joseph, in her normal voice.)* It is He who is responsible for your being cast back into the pit once again.

JOSEPH. The pit?

VASHNEE. Yes. The pit.

JOSEPH. Jehovah, stop her.

VASHNEE. I shall not kill you, Joseph. I only want to cool you off for a few years. *(Two Guards appear and advance on Joseph.)*

JOSEPH. *(Raises his hand high, with a garment of Vashnee still in each of his hands, and calls out to the heavens.)* Jehovah, why hast Thou raised me so high, only to cast me into the pit again?

VASHNEE. *(To the Guards.)* Take him away. The charge is rape. *(The Guards advance on Joseph as there is a sharp blackout.)*

End of Act I

86

ACT II

Scene 1

Reuben, the Narrator, is on stage playing the Pharaoh theme on his flute. The houselights dim down. Reuben stops playing and speaks to the audience.

REUBEN. Joseph was sentenced to five years in prison. There were many men in that prison, each heavy with the burden of his imprisonment. To lighten that burden, they took to imagining and dreaming. Some of the dreams they had at night, in sleep; and some they had during the day, sitting very still, their eyes open and glazed. After the dream, they would rise and say, "I had a dream. Who will interpret it for me?" Some of the other prisoners would gather around and take turns at interpreting. But none was so skilled as Joseph. He seemed to understand all three elements—the dreamer, the dream and the reason for the dream. After a time, knowledge of his skill spread even beyond the prison. . . . Joseph had been in prison for two years, when one morning the Pharaoh announced that he had had two dreams. He called for the prophets, the soothsayers and the interpreters of the land to come forward and explain his dreams. Many came before the Pharaoh because it was well known that he who pleased the Pharaoh would be greatly rewarded. And though it was equally well known that he who displeased the Pharaoh would be punished most severely, such is the combination of greed, confidence and hope, that each prophet, each soothsayer, each interpreter believed that assuredly he alone would interpret the Pharaoh's dreams to satisfaction—that while others would be condemned, he alone would receive the rich reward. *(Points to Rakaph, the Prophet, in the scene to be described shortly, and plays his flute as indicated.*

It is two years later.

The scene is the throne room of Pharaoh's palace. The Pharaoh theme is heard fully. Pharaoh sits immobile. His beard is golden in color and obviously false. It is a ceremonial beard, of the "spectacle-type", with wiring that hooks over the ears.

Malfi sits on the right side of the throne wearing the official outer robe and the golden collar of the Governor of Egypt. Rakaph, the Prophet, is interpreting Pharaoh's dreams.)

RAKAPH. *(Has a huge conch in his hand.)* And the Dispenser of the Seven Truths speaks further unto Rakaph, the Prophet, and says—*(Holds conch to his ear and listens intently. Reuben, off on one side of the stage, plays a thin tune, a variation of the Water theme.)*—the seven thin cows are the seven nations of the world—*(Reuben stops playing. Rakaph pauses, a look of dismay on his face.)*

PHARAOH. Go on, Rakaph. I'm listening.

RAKAPH. *(Shakes conch vigorously, puts it to his ear again. Reuben plays. Rakaph continues confidently.)*—and the seven nations will yet be conquered by mighty Egypt's armies, and by you, O mighty Pharaoh.

PHARAOH. You pander to my vanity.

RAKAPH. *(Puts conch to his ear. Rakaph's speech continues the rhythm of Reuben's flute.)* It is the truth as dispensed by the Dispenser of the Seven Truths—because your dream contained the holy number seven.

PHARAOH. Tell me, Malfi, are all his truths as true as this one?

RAKAPH. *(His speech continues to take on the rhythm of Reuben's flute. Reuben plays until indicated.)* The seven truths are equally true, O mighty Pharaoh. For no truth can be truer than these truths revealed by the Dispenser of the Seven Truths.

PHARAOH. I dare say. Just as no blessing can be more blessed than the blessing I must bless you with.

RAKAPH. *(Falls on his knees.)* But I am unworthy, O mighty Pharaoh!

PHARAOH. Most assuredly. Nevertheless, you shall feast on the bread of contentment—

RAKAPH. On the bread of contentment.

PHARAOH. —and be garbed in the robes of peace.

RAKAPH. *(Kisses Pharaoh's foot.)* In the robes of peace. Blessed be Pharaoh, who can comprehend the wisdom of the Seven Truths.

PHARAOH. It is the same wisdom that has taught me to reward you as I do now. *(He indicates to Malfi who*

89

strikes a rod against a copper sheet. An Executioner appears and moves to Rakaph. Reuben stops playing. He exits unobtrusively.)

RAKAPH. *(Throws himself at Pharaoh's feet.)* But you promised me a great blessing, O wise and just Pharaoh!

PHARAOH. You shall have it. On your tomb I will have inscribed the request for free passage of your soul on the roads of the hereafter.

RAKAPH. But this can't be. Pharaoh wishes to test his servant.

PHARAOH. No, Rakaph. This grinning truth called death is the truest of all truths. He has eaten every holy liar and every holy lie since the world began—and still he can swallow another. *(Malfi makes a gesture. The Executioner springs forward and drags Rakaph off.)*

MALFI. Pharaoh is himself today. He jests divinely.

PHARAOH. If I have pleased you, my satisfaction is complete.

MALFI. His greed for his reward was the best part.

PHARAOH. You knew what I intended?

MALFI. From the beginning.

PHARAOH. I must be more adroit next time. If the element of surprise is omitted, the amusement is blunted. *(Malfi claps his hands. Soft, low music is heard, the Pharaoh theme.)* I enjoy these pleasant interludes. *(Malfi claps his hands twice. A Footwasher appears and kneels before Pharaoh.)* Bring perfume of ambergris and roses and wash my feet where he that was, kissed me. I do not fancy the kisses of dead men. *(Footwasher goes quickly.)* Well, Malfi, shall we do another or shall we eat first?

MALFI. I think we should do one more so that Pharaoh will not be over-worked during the heat of the afternoon.

PHARAOH. Am I never to have any rest? At least, let us drink first. *(Malfi claps his hands. Sharshees, official wine keeper for Pharaoh, appears. He has a tendency to repeat phrases and bounce on his heels whenever he does so. He utters the words, "life-wealth-and-health" in a mechanical sing-song way, performing a short mechanical bow as he does so.)*

SHARSHEES. What wine will Pharaoh, life-wealth-and-health, drink?

PHARAOH. Some more of the amber-colored stuff.

SHARSHEES. Is Pharaoh, life-wealth-and-health, sure he wishes that? Yesterday, he said it reminded him of embalmer's fluid. *(Laughs weakly, terrified at his own audacity. He bows and goes. The Footwasher appears and washes Pharaoh's feet as Malfi and Pharaoh continue their conversation. When the Footwasher is finished, he goes.)*

MALFI. Pharaoh's jests are always irresistible.

PHARAOH. Rakaph didn't find us so funny.

MALFI. Poor fellow, he had no sense of humor.

PHARAOH. Have you, Malfi? How would you like to stand before me, interpret my dreams, and then go with my executioner?

MALFI. I'm no prophet, only Governor of Egypt. But if it will add to Pharaoh's amusement, I'll go with his executioner gladly.

91

ACT II

PHARAOH. Nobly spoken, Malfi. Perhaps it is you who should be having his head chopped off instead of these poor, deluded fellows. For it is your miserable management that has brought Egypt to the wretched state in which she finds herself. . . . Do you wonder why I chop off the heads of the poor prophets and let yours rest comfortably on your shoulders? Well, Malfi, you are one of the few people I find more amusing alive than dead.

MALFI. It's fortunate for me that Pharaoh finds me amusing.

PHARAOH. You lack but one thing to make you the perfect Governor of Egypt.

MALFI. What is this one thing, Pharaoh? I shall possess it tomorrow.

PHARAOH. Some little understanding of the elementary principles of governing a nation such as Egypt. This, you lack entirely. Otherwise, you're a fine fellow and perfectly suited for your job. *(Sharshees appears with the wine, tastes it and hands the cup to Pharaoh, who drinks from it.)* By the way, Sharshees, where is that Hebrew interpreter of dreams that you were so eloquent about? *(Malfi listens closely with an expression of alarm.)*

SHARSHEES. Be not angry with your slave. The Hebrew comes—he comes.

PHARAOH. You said that three executions ago.

SHARSHEES. We have just brought him from prison. The delay is only a matter of bathing and purifying him before he enters the royal presence—the royal presence.

PHARAOH. You didn't bathe and purify those other prophets who were here.

SHARSHEES. They were all holy men, O Pharaoh, life-weath-and-health. It's against their religion to bathe.

PHARAOH. Has this Hebrew no religion? How do you know you haven't washed off all the sacred magic that clung to him?

SHARSHEES. Pharaoh, life-weath-and-health, will see for himself. Ah, he will prophesy beautifully, beautifully.

PHARAOH. He will have to. Otherwise his career as a prophet will be a short one.

SHARSHEES. And I ordered him bathed and perfumed and dressed in a manner befitting his appearance before you—appearance before you.

PHARAOH. Such extravagance. Have you no regard for the royal treasury—the royal treasury?

SHARSHEES. Pharaoh, life-wealth-and-health, is pleased to jest.

PHARAOH. All that gold wasted for one appearance.

SHARSHEES. One? Pharaoh, life-wealth-and-health, is sure even before he has heard him—even before he has heard him? But he will prophesy beautifully, for he is a clever lad—a clever lad—a very clever lad.

PHARAOH. It wasn't the fly in the wine that sent you to prison, but your damnable habit of singing a chorus to yourself as you jump about. Prepare for a big jump directly to my friend, the executioner. Since you summoned the Hebrew before me, if he dies, you die too. (Sharshees goes miserably.)

MALFI. The only Hebrew I ever knew was a revolting creature.

93

PHARAOH. Is this the wild desert tribe that perform the curious anatomical religious rites upon themselves?

MALFI. Yes. They are a degraded and savage people. If I were Pharaoh, I would waste no time on this one.

PHARAOH. But I must talk to him. A king must know everything. I want to question him about those tribal customs. It must be terrible to be shorn of your pride. Is all the joy of life cut off at one fell stroke? And if so, why do they decapitate themselves in this fashion?

MALFI. I shall endeavor to secure accurate information on this point for Pharaoh at the earliest opportunity.

PHARAOH. Perhaps the next prophet, who snorts so impatiently, can tell me. He ought to know something useful—with all that dirt on him. (Claps his hands. The music, which has been heard faintly and intermittently, stops.) Our pleasant interlude comes to an end. (Shilah, a dirty old man, naked except for a coarse black robe and girdle, comes in briskly. His coarse black hair hangs to his shoulders. He jerks his head wildly as he talks; his eyes glitter vividly. He comes forward, bowing perfunctorily to Pharaoh, and starts off at a great speed, working into a frenzy.)

SHILAH. Shilah, the Soothsayer, am I. I stem from a long line of soothsayers. It was told by the father of the father of my father to the father of my father. And the father of my father has told it to my father and my father has told it to me, and now I tell it to you, O Pharaoh.

PHARAOH. I see. It is venerable, therefore valuable.

SHILAH. (Rushing on.) When I heard your dream, O King, long did I invoke the gods.

94

PHARAOH. Yes, yes—and what did they say?

SHILAH. *(Chanting, falls to his knees and bows in each direction.)*
And I bowed my head to the north,
And I bowed my head to the east,
And I bowed my head to the south,
And I bowed my head to the west.

PHARAOH. How fortunate there are no more points to the earth.

SHILAH. And I buried my body in the holy sands so that naught but my nostrils and eyes remained above. And so buried, I studied the skies for the holy signs of the Trinity of the Bat and the Boar and the Gazelle, and the holy truth that the trinity of the Bat and the Boar and the Gazelle stand guard over by day and by night.

PHARAOH. It had better be a meaty truth—or he will have to bow his head again.

SHILAH. *(Over-riding Pharaoh and going on at a great pace.)* There is no truth but the truth of the Trinity of the Bat and the Boar and the Gazelle. The fat sleek cows are Egypt and the storm beaten wheat is the world. Egypt will destroy the world as the cows ate the wheat in your dreams, and Egypt will prosper as other nations fall.

PHARAOH. Don't you know that no nation can prosper with the rest of the world in ruins?

SHILAH. That is no concern of mine. I speak revealed truth.

PHARAOH. Egypt is a nation of traders. With whom can we trade if other nations are destroyed?

SHILAH. *(Continues unheeding.)* The truth of the Bat

and the Boar and the Gazelle goes on to say that the entire world will be one great Egypt and that—

PHARAOH. A pretty dream and a still prettier interpretation. Very sensible of the cows in your dream to eat the wheat. The crazy cows in my dream didn't eat the wheat; they ate each other. But I suppose that's no concern of yours either?

SHILAH. It is not I that speak, Pharaoh, but the Bat, the Boar and the Gazelle. *(Prostrates himself before the throne.)*

PHARAOH. Then the Bat and the Boar and the Gazelle will have their eloquence amputated and not you. *(Malfi strikes the copper. The Executioner appears and drags Shilah off, as Pharaoh continues talking.)* Will no one satisfy me? I am overworked and so are my executioners. Soon they will begin to complain. And if they complain I will have to have them executed too. But who will execute the executioners? I must find someone to interpret my dreams. *(Sharshees enters with Joseph and moves forward.)* Is that your Hebrew, Sharshees? *(Joseph, clad in rags, stands before the throne. Malfi is very perturbed.)*

SHARSHEES. Have mercy, Pharaoh, life-wealth-and-health. It's not my fault that he comes like this. I tried to purify him.

PHARAOH. You've caught the fish. Leave the cleaning and cooking to me. *(Joseph deliberately ascends the steps toward the throne, takes the wand and strikes the gong. Pharaoh makes no move. Joseph points to himself as the Executioner appears.)*

JOSEPH. Take me away!

96

PHARAOH. I see that you don't understand the principles of sound government. If people are to be allowed to walk in here and order their own heads cut off, what's the sense of having a king?

JOSEPH. Well, what *is* the sense, if he can't cut off a head without discussing it for an hour?

PHARAOH. Even a king must breathe between executions. And who are you to complain? You haven't amused us yet.

JOSEPH. No. But I have listened to one of Pharaoh's jests. Must I listen to another? Is there no justice here?

PHARAOH. No king can afford the luxury of justice . . . . A strange fellow, this Hebrew. We must have him prophesy. . . . If you interpret my dreams as honestly as my jests, you shall receive great reward.

JOSEPH. I will try. *(Waves the Executioner off.)* Let us accept for the moment, merely for the sake of the prophecy, that you actually did dream those dreams. Then I would say— *(Assumes the stance and tone of a professional soothsayer and plunges ahead.)* —the two dreams are one. The fat cows and the fine ears of corn represent seven years of great prosperity for Egypt. The lean cows and blasted ears of corn represent years of hunger which will follow the seven fat years. The lean will swallow the fat. There will be only hunger. *(Stares pointedly at Malfi.)* Where are your administrators? Have they no foresight, no concern for the future? Why are they not building granaries to store the wheat of the fat years in order to tide Egypt over the lean? . . . This is what I would tell if it were a dream.

ACT II

PHARAOH. Marvelous. Come forward so that I may have a better look at you. *(Joseph moves closer.)* I am very taken with your idea of building granaries.

JOSEPH. I like it myself.

PHARAOH. We must talk further on it.

JOSEPH. *(Shrewdly.)* But the fact is, I do not believe that Pharaoh dreamt those dreams. You invented them. For you are troubled, Pharaoh—sorely troubled about the state of affairs in Egypt.

PHARAOH. Marvelous. Marvelous.

JOSEPH. In this dream you invented, the fat cows and fine ears of corn are your symbols for the prosperity Egypt enjoyed when Pharaoh had wise counsellors to advise him.

PHARAOH. This fellow sees through everything.

JOSEPH. The lean cows and blasted ears of corn are the evil times that Pharaoh foresees as a result of the unwise counsel of his present advisors.

PHARAOH. This becomes more and more amazing. He can read even your mind, Malfi. *(To Joseph.)* Tell me the secret of your power, Hebrew. Is it a revelation from the gods?

JOSEPH. How much of such matters we owe to God and how much to ourselves, is a question on which I should like Malfi's opinion.

MALFI. There is nothing miraculous about his superficial knowledge, Pharaoh.

PHARAOH. It's comforting to know that it's merely

98

superficial. I was beginning to fear that he might really know what he was talking about.

MALFI. He has been in a position to pick up court gossip, which he uses for his own advantage.

PHARAOH. Then you know him?

MALFI. Only too well. He was once a slave in Potiphar's house—and for a brief time, Chamberlain to Potiphar. But he committed an unmentionable crime.

PHARAOH. What! This is not the fellow who raped Vashnee?

JOSEPH. I see that my crime is not as unmentionable as Malfi would have you believe.

PHARAOH. Oh, we talk about everything here. And crimes of passion have a peculiar fascination for me. Of course, I think they're practically always inexcusable. With a little patience you can usually accomplish your purpose without all this barbaric violence.

JOSEPH. I will remember that, Pharaoh, the next time I feel the urge coming over me.

PHARAOH. We will discuss this further at our leisure . . . . But just now there is another matter that seems more urgent. Tell me, Hebrew, do you know anything about this new science of government which every fool is prattling about?

JOSEPH. I governed Egypt for two years.

PHARAOH. Strange. I don't recall your administration. In just what period of Egypt's history did your reign occur?

JOSEPH. In the period immediately preceding the Great Rape.

PHARAOH. But at this time Potiphar— *(Stops abruptly, astonished. Then in a changed tone, with marked interest.)* So *you* were the real governor of Egypt all that time?

JOSEPH. I did what I could through Potiphar. Even Pharaoh must have noticed a change for the worse after my unmentionable crime.

PHARAOH. Decidedly. I remember wondering what had happened to Potiphar's brain. From the day Vashnee was raped, it seemed to go to smash completely. I got rid of him and appointed Malfi. But there must have been an unmentionable crime in Malfi's family also.

JOSEPH. *(Making a sign of cutting a throat.)* You got rid of Potiphar?

PHARAOH. No. No. Potiphar belongs to one of our first families. I gently shifted him into an insignificant position with a high-sounding title. I got Potiphar a job as one of the many assistants to the All-High Priest and Defender of the Faith.

JOSEPH. Oh!

PHARAOH. His fishing continues to improve. He has won first prize in the annual tournament two years in succession. *(Princess Asenath rushes forward excitedly. She has matured into a beautiful young woman.)*

ASENATH. Joseph!

JOSEPH. Asenath!

ASENATH. Joseph. I thought you were dead.

JOSEPH. *(Moved.)* Asenath, my dear Asenath, why are you here? *(Murmuring.)* The bud has burst into bloom.

ASENATH. I came because I heard you were alive. When my father told me you were dead, I wept for many days.

JOSEPH. This morning I too thought I was dead. But now I should like to live again.

PHARAOH. That is a dangerous admission to make, Hebrew. As long as living meant nothing to you, you were a free man. But now I have your neck under my yoke like all the others.

ASENATH. *(Alarmed, clinging to his hand.)* What does he mean, Joseph? He won't harm you?

JOSEPH. I think not—as long as he finds me useful.

PHARAOH. And amusing. A rare combination in a statesman. Have no fear, Princess. He shall live. I will not allow the royal physician within ten cubits of him.

ASENATH. Oh, thank you, Pharaoh. I did not understand.

PHARAOH. Very few people do understand me when I talk, but I've discovered that it doesn't really make the slightest difference. How old are you, Princess?

ASENATH. Fifteen—almost. I'll be fifteen when the Nile rises again.

PHARAOH. Fifteen. An exquisite age. The Nile must be impatient to celebrate it. I shall expect floods.

ASENATH. If Pharaoh is pleased, I am happy. *(Bows, looks warmly at Joseph, then moves aside.)*

PHARAOH. Hebrew! For a man of your reputation and

instincts, you restrain your barbaric passions admirably. And I believe that you actually outblushed the Princess.

JOSEPH. I was thinking of my unmentionable crime against her mother.

PHARAOH. That must be charged to youth and inexperience. *(Breaking off.)* But I have another concern now. *(Raises his voice and calls ominously.)* Let Potiphar, the priest, come forward.

GUARD. *(Calls out.)* Let Potiphar, the priest, come forward.

POTIPHAR. *(Dressed in ecclesiastical robes enters and comes to the foot of the dais.)* Pharaoh's servant is here.

PHARAOH. Did you throw the best brain in Egypt into a dungeon merely because you observed some slight emotional irregularity in its owner?

POTIPHAR. The irregularity was *not* slight. This man violated my wife.

PHARAOH. Is that a legitimate excuse for giving Egypt the kind of government she has had to put up with for the past two years?

POTIPHAR. I had to defend the honor and sanctity of my home. What would people have said if I hadn't?

PHARAOH. Nothing comparable to what they would say now could they grasp the true magnitude of your stupidity. But I'll rectify your blunder. *(Waves Potiphar to one side and calls out.)* Let the Princess Asenath come forward once more. And let Lady Vashnee enter, and let her also come forward. *(Vashnee enters from an outer chamber. She and Asenath approach Pharaoh. He waves Vashnee*

102

Scene 1

to stand by the side of Potiphar and waves Asenath to stand by the side of Joseph. He studies the two groups, pleased with the effect. To Joseph.) Hebrew, I— (Breaks off.) By the way, what is your name?

JOSEPH. Joseph.

PHARAOH. Joseph, I pronounce your blood, royal blood. And I give you Princess Asenath, daughter of Potiphar and Vashnee, for wife.

ASENATH. (Kneels at Joseph's feet.) Seven times and seven times at the feet of my lord I bow. I am thy servant forever. (Kisses his hand. Joseph gently withdraws it and raises her.)

JOSEPH. So now you have become my mother-in-law.

VASHNEE. Thief. You have used me. You have stolen my idea of the granaries.

JOSEPH. Jehovah must have put the words in my mouth.

VASHNEE. Jehovah. Jehovah. What a convenience He is for you.

PHARAOH. Now, wait. Let's see. There was something else. Oh, yes, I remember. I proclaim you Governor of Egypt.

MALFI. (Takes off the official outer robe and the golden collar of the Governor of Egypt, and hands them to Joseph, who puts them on. He cries out tragi-comically.) An hour ago I was Governor of Egypt. What happened to me? (Bewildered, he moves off to the side.)

PHARAOH. (To Joseph, pointing to Malfi's chair.) You will sit there. And I warn you, I shall do precisely what you tell me, and see that everybody else does the same,

103

so if it happens to be wrong, you'll have no one to blame but yourself. *(Joseph attempts to say something, but Pharaoh cuts him off and continues.)* One thing more. Avoid as you would the plague this damnable habit of stringing words together endlessly. I acquired it from years of association with politicians. What I want from you is not words, but action. I can talk enough for both of us. *(With Pharaoh still talking, there is a complete blackout, replaced immediately by the deep blue-green light. In this light all the characters move off.)*

Scene 2

There is no pause in the action. A spotlight picks up Reuben, the Narrator, as he comes before the audience. He plays on his flute, then speaks to the audience.

REUBEN. Ten years have passed. The first seven of those ten were years of plenty. The harvests came full and rich, and Joseph, who had built thousands of granaries, collected a fifth part of the crop as a tax for the Pharaoh. The people did not grumble, for the earth brought forth by handfuls.

Then came the lean years. The first year, the waters of the Nile did not rise high enough and by midsummer, the crops had shrivelled as though placed in a hot oven. The next year the Nile rose too high and in its embrace swept away all the rich soil, depositing it in the bottom of the river. This is the third year that there will be disaster in the fields in place of harvest. And it is not alone in Egypt that the crops have failed; hunger stalks the world.

In that first year of failure, Joseph let it be known that there was corn for sale. Soon Egypt became the granary for the world. Caravans poured in from the four corners of the earth. Joseph made the Pharaoh the richest king since the beginning of time.

As for us in Canaan, first we ate the surplus, then we were forced to eat our seed corn, and then we gathered together our money and journeyed to Egypt to buy corn. *(The light on Reuben fades. He moves off the stage. The light is replaced by the lighting required for the scene. It is ten years later.*

The scene is Joseph's office in the Governor's palace. There is the Governor's chair, a smaller chair and a desk. Off to the side is a large sketch lying face down. There is a pitcher of wine and four goblets.

Joseph, wearing the golden collar of the Governor of Egypt, radiates energy and power. Three men are with him; one an armed warrior, the other two are engineers. One of the Engineers is an older, sober man, staid and solid; the other, his assistant, is young, friendly, optimistic. The four are just finishing a conference. Maps and plans are spread out on the table. There is a sense of satisfaction, excitement, celebration.)

JOSEPH. It is a beautiful plan, my good engineers. I toast you for it. *(He takes the pitcher of wine with the intention of filling the four goblets. But he is so permeated by the excitement of the hour that as he starts to pour he becomes involved with the conversation, moves away from the goblets, goes back to them again, moves away from them again.)*

1ST ENGINEER. Thank you, Excellency. But the plans are almost as much yours as ours.

JOSEPH. No. No. The work is yours. I make a toast to our time—to our time and the tasks of our time. We have the engineering capacity to harness the Nile, to eliminate hunger. And as we banish hunger, so will we teach the people to depend not on magic and miracles of priests, but on the miracles of work which they themselves perform. *(He has at last poured the wine. They raise their goblets.)* To a world without hunger! *(The four drink the toast.)* I want to tell you a parable. When my father, Jacob, was a young man he had to flee from his home, pursued by the wrath of his brother, Esau. He fled to Mesopotamia, and came to Padan-Aram where Laban, his uncle, lived. He stayed with Laban, working for him as a shepherd. Laban had two daughters; the older was Leah, the younger Rachel. It was said that Leah was tender-eyed, but Rachel, my mother, was beautiful and well formed. It is true that Rachel was beautiful, and most beautiful of all were her clear, grey eyes. As for Leah—tender-eyed? From this you might have the impression that Leah's eyes were kind and gentle. The fact is that Leah was a homely woman, with a most homely face. And those eyes! They did not look together at an object and they were small and red-rimmed and they teared constantly.

And Jacob loved Rachel, the younger of the two, and said to Laban, "I will serve thee seven years for Rachel, thy younger daughter." And so it was. And Jacob labored seven years and they seemed unto him but a few days, for the love he had for Rachel. Jacob said, "My seven years are fulfilled. Give me my wife that I may go in unto her." Laban made a wedding feast and in the night after the feast, Jacob's bride was brought to him. She was wearing the traditional heavy veil so that none could see through it, and she maintained the traditional silence required of a bride, uttering not a single word.

107

And Jacob went into the tent and he took pleasure with her that night.

But in the dawn, as the light filtered into the tent, his joy turned to sand in his mouth as he saw the beauty of Rachel turn into the homeliness of Leah; as he saw the grey eyes of Rachel turn into the small, red-rimmed eyes of Leah.

Jacob rose hastily from the tent and sought out his uncle, father-in-law, Laban, and cried out with a great shout, "Why have you deceived me? Did I not work seven years for Rachel?" "Not so," answered Laban, smooth as rain water mixed with honey, "I have not deceived you, my dear son-in-law. You do not know the ways of our land even though you have lived here for seven years. It is not our custom to give the younger and the elder not yet married—and I am a man of custom in my country."

The tears were in Jacob's eyes. He shouted unto Laban, "How can I gain Rachel for wife?" Laban answered, smooth as rain water mixed with honey, "You have labored seven years for your first bride. Labor seven more and I will give you Rachel into your hand." And so it was agreed. Jacob labored another seven years for Rachel.

I did not want to build the Leah granaries; I wanted to build the Rachel dams. But I knew that first I must insure my favor with the Pharaoh—enhance the power of the Pharaoh. A statesman maneuvers; *I* maneuvered. For seven years I have built the Leah granaries with my heart always bent to the Rachel dams. Now the seven Leah years, the granary years, have passed. I have made the Pharaoh the ruler of the richest and most powerful nation in the world.

SCENE 2

1ST ENGINEER. You have earned the right to work on your dams.

JOSEPH. I have earned the right, and I have the power and organization to do so.

2ND ENGINEER. Only the priesthood will not be happy about the dams but they will have no grounds to complain.

JOSEPH. When the dams are completed I shall declare a Jubilee Year—(*Shows them the sketch which has been lying face down, depicting Pharaoh, heroic in size, standing athwart a dam and all around him are fields of corn, barley and wheat, huge stalks which reach to his shoulders.*) A Jubilee in honor of the Pharaoh who turned a strip of desert, and more, and yet more, into green fields. Always adding to the bloom of this golden country. A Jubilee Year to honor the Pharaoh. . . . How quickly can you put the plan into operation?

1ST ENGINEER. Everything is ready. Affix your seal and the work begins at dawn tomorrow.

JOSEPH. (*2nd Engineer and Warrior hold several plans as Joseph rolls some soft clay between his fingers and then places it on the plans. Takes off his signet ring and places it on the clay.*) At dawn tomorrow we begin building the new Egypt. (*The Warrior signals. The First Guard appears, takes the plans and goes. Joseph, at desk, studying several plans with the two Engineers.*) You estimate that it will take three years to complete the dams?

1ST ENGINEER. That is so, your Excellency.

JOSEPH. Three years. Three years. (*Moves impatiently,*

109

absorbed in his reflections.) Our time will not wait. . . . Time—you are my enemy! . . . If I could bring about the change overnight so that when the sun rises it would rise on the new Egypt, Egypt golden and fruitful!

1ST ENGINEER. People and work make dams, Excellency—not magic and miracles. And that takes time.

JOSEPH. *(With a touch of sadness.)* Ay—well—. Time. Time. Time. Will I be able to complete the task of my generation? *(Suddenly matter-of-fact, precise and brisk.)* You have work to do. You may go. Farewell.

WARRIOR AND TWO ENGINEERS. Farewell, Excellency. *(They leave. Joseph studies the plans. The Second Guard enters.)*

SECOND GUARD. Your Excellency, they have arrived. The Hebrews from Canaan whom you told us to watch for, have arrived.

JOSEPH. Where are they now?

SECOND GUARD. The soldiers are holding them at the gates.

JOSEPH. They do not suspect that the order to detain them comes from me?

SECOND GUARD. No.

JOSEPH. Bring them here at once.

SECOND GUARD. Yes, Excellency. *(Second Guard goes. Joseph, alone, paces in excitement.)*

FIRST GUARD. *(Enters, in sonorous tones.)* His Eminence, the All-High Priest of the Sun God and Defender of the Public Faith! *(There is a fanfare. It is the Potiphar theme, but now has a strong touch of the ecclesiastical.)*

SCENE 2

POTIPHAR. *(Enters dressed in splendid ecclesiastical robes.)* Well, well, how are you, dear son-in-law? *(First Guard goes.)*

JOSEPH. *(Looks at him in astonishment. Joseph is involved with the news of his brothers' arrival and in the beginning of the scene does not realize the full significance of the ecclesiastical robes on Potiphar.)* Speechless in the presence of so much magnificence, my dear father-in-law.

POTIPHAR. It is rather splendid, don't you think?

JOSEPH. Dazzling. But how is it that you are wearing the robes of the All-High Priest?

POTIPHAR. *(Preening.)* I am the All-High Priest. This morning the former All-High Priest was assassinated by some lunatic who had paid him for a charm that didn't work. Vashnee and I were having breakfast with the Pharaoh when the news was brought.

JOSEPH. Vashnee?

POTIPHAR. Yes. Immediately the Pharaoh said that for a long time he had been wanting to reward me for my years of devoted and, if I may quote him, valuable service, and what better way than to advance me to the position of All-High Priest. Though there was a little hitch for a few moments. Vashnee didn't want me to take the job. I nudged her, even gave her a little kick, but she held firm.

JOSEPH. Nevertheless, I see you wearing the robes of the All-High Priest.

POTIPHAR. Vashnee knew I had my heart set on the job for some time and she didn't want me to be disap-

111

pointed. So she came up with an excellent idea. She said she would reluctantly allow me to take the job, provided the Pharaoh would appoint her High Priestess so that she could stand side by side with me and share my danger.

JOSEPH. So Vashnee was appointed High Priestess?

POTIPHAR. Pharaoh was most reluctant, but she held firm to her condition. She can push hard—but this morning—oh! Finally the Pharaoh gave her the necessary permission. Side by side with me she stands.

JOSEPH. Where is she now?

POTIPHAR. Well, I was just leading up to—

JOSEPH. Where is Vashnee?

POTIPHAR. Vashnee said there was no use my coming here to talk with you. But I felt that I should come and hear from you directly that the story she heard is not true.

JOSEPH. Where is Vashnee?

POTIPHAR. She's gone to the temple for her ceremonial beard of office.

JOSEPH. Why bother with a beard of office just to talk with me?

POTIPHAR. That's exactly what I told her. But she said —and I quote her, "I wouldn't dream of facing Joseph without the aid of all the accoutrements of my office." So off she went to the temple for her beard.

JOSEPH. Out with it.

POTIPHAR. Vashnee heard an incredible story about you, Joseph. Some wild talk about your planning to build dams along the Nile—on the holy river Nile, mind you!

Scene 2

JOSEPH. Fantastic, isn't it?

POTIPHAR. *(Relieved.)* There! I knew it couldn't b
true.

JOSEPH. *(Holding up the plans.)* My engineers start work
tomorrow.

POTIPHAR. Then Vashnee was right. *(Joseph nods.)* If
you start work on the dams, the gods in their wrath will
strike you down.

JOSEPH. Then you should encourage me. When a bolt
of lightning strikes me dead, the priests of Egypt can point
me out as an example for future blasphemers. Faith would
be rekindled and the coffers of your temples would be
filled.

POTIPHAR. There is the slight chance that the gods
might overlook what you're doing this time. Then what
would happen to Egypt?

JOSEPH. You mean, what would happen to the priests.

POTIPHAR. What would happen to religion?

JOSEPH. You mean, what would happen to your income.

POTIPHAR. When wine is placed into barrels, have you
noticed how the wood becomes wine-soaked? When hay
is stored in a barn, have you noticed how stalks cling to
the walls? Much gold passes through our hands—naturally,
some of it sticks to our palms. We always have enough
to give to our friends and well-wishers.

JOSEPH. And you want me to be your well-wisher?

POTIPHAR. As I want to be yours. You should look to
your future. Accumulate some *personal* wealth. Besides,

113

it's all very nice to show an interest—but after all, they are the common people. It's the natural order for us to have the best. Any man who tries to fly in the face of nature is a fool.

JOSEPH. You're looking at such a fool now.

POTIPHAR. Take care, Joseph, my good son in law. We have power.

JOSEPH. You'll need it, my good father-in-law.

POTIPHAR. I thought I could reason with you. Vashnee was right. (He goes. The First and Second Guard enter.)

SECOND GUARD. Your Excellency, I have brought the Hebrews.

JOSEPH. Where are they?

SECOND GUARD. In the ante-room.

JOSEPH. Bring them in. Let them wait for me here. (Joseph goes off into the inner chamber of the palace. The Second Guard returns to the door and signals Joseph's brothers. They enter. They are worn. Time has not used them easily; some of them are gray, others graying. Their rude shepherds' clothing contrasts sharply with the sumptuous surroundings. They enter hesitantly, looking about in open-eyed wonder.)

SECOND GUARD. You are to wait until his Excellency returns.

GAD. Not a bad little tent. I could use one like it myself.

DAN. While you're at it, get one for me too.

REUBEN. Why does this great lord of Egypt send for us?

114

FIRST GUARD. His Excellency, the Governor of Egypt. *(Joseph enters. He has put on the official outer robe of the Governor of Egypt. He is also wearing a hood-like arrangement which partially conceals his face. He carries in his hand three small bags of gold. The brothers kneel, bowing their heads to the ground. Joseph ascends the dais to his chair. He sits, putting the three bags of gold by his side.)*

JOSEPH. *(Roughly to the Guards.)* Who are these men? What are they doing here?

THE BROTHERS. *(Their speeches follow each other rapidly, even overlap.)*
  REUBEN: You sent for us, great Lord.
  ASHER: Canaan is a land of hunger.
  LEVI: All we want is corn.
  GAD: And we pay for what we buy.
  ZEBULUN: We must eat.

FIRST GUARD. Silence. Do not speak until you are spoken to.

SECOND GUARD. These are the Hebrews from Canaan whom your Excellency wished to question.

JOSEPH. *(To Guards).* Go. *(The Guards leave.)* My messengers tell me that you are spies. To seek out the nakedness of the land have you come.

THE BROTHERS.
  REUBEN: We are honest shepherds.
  SIMEON: Ten children of one father.
  ASHER: All we want is food.
  REUBEN: The only place in the world that has corn is Egypt.

ISSACHER: Our money is in our sacks.

DAN: No spies. We're honest shepherds.

ZEBULUN: What harm can shepherds do to a great country like Egypt?

NAPHTALI: Starving children.

REUBEN: Only to buy corn for our starving families.

JOSEPH. So—you are honest shepherds and you have come to buy corn.

REUBEN. By our God and the head of our father, we swear it.

JOSEPH. By the head of your father? Your father—your father is dead?

REUBEN. No. Our father is alive. He is aged, but he is alive.

JOSEPH. What is his name?

REUBEN. Jacob.

JOSEPH. Jacob. Jacob. Jacob. Is he well? Tell me, is he well?

REUBEN. Yes. He is well.

JOSEPH. How have you left him?

REUBEN. The food that was left was enough for the father and the households, but not enough for us to have stayed.

JOSEPH. Tell me, honest shepherds, in your own country at harvest, when you have been in the fields binding sheaves, have you ever seen a sheaf of wheat—(*Rises sharply from his chair.*) —stand up suddenly as I am standing now, while all the other sheaves bow down before it, as you are bowing to me? *(The brothers lift their heads in astonishment.)*

GAD. What did you say, great Lord?

JOSEPH. You are not deaf. You heard what I said.

GAD. Canaan is no heathen land. Our sheaves are not possessed of evil spirits. Do they jump in Egypt?

JOSEPH. Like grasshoppers—since Egypt *is* a heathen land. *(The brothers exchange uneasy glances.)* You say you are all the sons of one father. How many of you are there?

REUBEN. We are eleven, great Lord. But the youngest is home with the father.

JOSEPH. Eleven. Are there stars in your country?

REUBEN. *(Startled.)* Stars?

JOSEPH. At night, in clear weather, are the heavens filled with stars—myriads of them?

REUBEN. There are stars everywhere, great Lord.

JOSEPH. Have you ever seen a family of eleven great ones marching across the sky?

REUBEN. Every night in fair weather. When we are in the plains with our sheep, we mark direction by them.

JOSEPH. Once there was a twelfth—a little one, but his big brothers became jealous of him and plucked him from the great space and threw him— *(Breaks off.)* Where did they throw him? Do any of you know?

THE BROTHERS. *(Whisper to each other; the speeches follow rapidly.)*

REUBEN. Jehovah has sent this punishment upon us.

117

SIMEON: This man is a sorcerer.

LEVI: He is possessed of a demon.

ZEBULUN: We are all dead men.

ISSACHER: Our sin has found us out.

REUBEN. Only Jehovah can help us now.

JOSEPH. Why do you whisper among yourselves? And your faces—your faces have the look of murderers.

GAD. No, great Lord. Our faces always look like this when we see strange things.

JOSEPH. If you had seen these stars do what I have seen, then you might speak of strange things.

GAD. What have you seen, great Lord?

JOSEPH. I have seen the eleven great stars bow down to the empty place where their lost brother sat. And I have seen the little lost brother rise up in wrath and hurl his big brothers into the great pit in the center of the earth.

GAD. A pit? Did you say a pit, great Lord?

JOSEPH. Yes—as deep as the earth—and filled with harmless vipers. *(Throws back his hood and reveals his face. Then he lets slip from his shoulders the official outer robe of the Governor of Egypt to reveal a garment very reminiscent of the coat of many colors.)*

THE BROTHERS. *(Together.)* Joseph!

JOSEPH. Well, brothers, how is it with you now?

REUBEN. We are caught in the trap of our own making.

JOSEPH. Not you, Reuben. You tried to save me. No matter what happens to the others, you are safe.

ZEBULUN. Let us live, Joseph.

118

ISSACHER. Forgive us for the harm we have done you.

GAD. *(Rises.)* I didn't harm you, brother. I'm the man who saved you—with Jehovah's help.

JOSEPH. Saved me! You?

GAD. *(With growing boldness.)* Me and Jehovah—yes. When I fished you out of the pit and sold you to the Ishmaelite, I was merely an instrument of Jehovah. *(Answering Joseph's incredulous look.)* Jehovah was working His wondrous ways through me. *(With an impertinent undertone.)* Not many boys starting where you did have their bottoms on a throne.

JOSEPH. *(Laughs.)* Everybody seems to be calling on You, Jehovah, to explain his conduct.

GAD. *(The brothers join in the laughter, though tentatively. One by one, they rise.)* It's our little brother, Joseph. Who does he think he is, trying to scare us this way?

JOSEPH. *(Cutting into their laughter.)* When you speak to the Governor of Egypt, you remain kneeling until you are given permission to rise. *(Their laughter ceases abruptly. They kneel, their heads low.)*

REUBEN. We bend our necks.

JOSEPH. You sold me for twenty pieces of silver. My brothers, that Ishmaelite slave-driver cheated you. I will make up your loss. Gold—not silver. *(With anger and contempt, forcefully throws the bags of gold in their midst.)* And why are you grovelling before me while I tower above you as Governor of Egypt? Because I dared to dream dreams and had the audacity to make them come true. I stand before you the life-giver. If I allow you to buy corn,

119

you live. If I refuse you—you, your children, the whole seed of Abraham, Isaac and Jacob, all, all but myself, all perish.

REUBEN. *(Rises. Picks up a sack of gold.)* Though I tried to save you, I well understood why they *had* to throw you into the pit. A young tyrant who never wanted to be with us, but always above us—with his dreams of ruling. They didn't sell you for the silver; they sold you to get rid of you. . . . Stand up, brothers. I was with you then; I am with them now. *(The brothers rise, one by one.)* Here is your gold. We want none of it. *(Throws the sack at Joseph's feet. Two of the other brothers pick up the other sacks and fling them at Joseph. Reuben comes close to Joseph.)* We are alone. Your guards are not here. They could not come in time to help you. With one turn of my wrist I could break your neck. *(The brothers move in on Joseph with menacing attitudes. Joseph shows his fear. Reuben stops them with a sharp gesture. He moves away from Joseph, the brothers following him.)* Do with us what you will. Turn us into carrion or slaves. We are not afraid of you. *(They stand apart, in a body.)*

JOSEPH. *(Sinks into the Governor's chair. He covers his face with his hands. There is a moment of silence. Then Joseph claps twice. The two Guards enter. There is a further moment of silence.)* Let the Hebrews buy their corn in peace. Then give them safe conduct to the borders of Egypt. *(The Second Guard leads the brothers off in silence. Joseph signals to the First Guard, who remains behind.)* Pick up this gold. In the mouth of each sack of corn they buy, place a gold coin. *(The Guard picks up the gold and goes. Joseph slumps in the Governor's chair.)* Why did I

120

taunt them? Why did I make them grovel before me? For revenge? They are hungered and weary, and grown old. Why didn't I go down and embrace them? Give them forgiveness—and ask for their forgiveness? *(There are tears in his eyes. He weeps silently.)*

FIRST GUARD. *(Enters.)* The Lord of both lands, loved of Ra, favorite of Mentu, the Lord of Thebes, of Amun and the Isles of the Sea, his Majesty, Pharaoh, anointed of Isis, King of Egypt. *(There is a fanfare. It is very grand; it combines the Pharaoh, Vashnee and Potiphar themes. Joseph rises wearily, puts on the outer robe of the Governor of Egypt. Pharaoh enters wearing his spectacle-type beard. He is followed in single file by Potiphar and then Vashnee who are also wearing spectacle-type beards. Vashnee wears the splendid robes of High Priestess. The two ecclesiastical robes complement each other in color and design. The First Guard goes.)*

PHARAOH. Well, Joseph, how are you?

JOSEPH. *(Rises. With tremendous effort he gathers his energy.)* I am well, Pharaoh. And yourself?

PHARAOH. I can tell you better after this conference of ours. *(Vashnee moves to Joseph. They study each other, faces very close.)*

JOSEPH. When we first met in the dungeon, did you think this would come to pass?

VASHNEE. If I did, do you think I would have let you get out of there alive? With my own hands I would have cut your throat.

PHARAOH. Shall we proceed to business? *(Pharaoh makes a move to seat himself on the small chair to the right of*

121

the Governor's chair. Joseph offers him the Governor's chair.)

JOSEPH. I think Pharaoh will find this more comfortable.

PHARAOH. No. You are the real ruler of Egypt and I have no desire to usurp your throne in a crisis such as this.

JOSEPH. I was not aware of any crisis.

PHARAOH. Neither was I—until the High Priestess informed me. *(Seats himself in the chair he originally chose.)* In so far as such a thing is possible, I shall change from a Pharaoh, a king, a god, to an ordinary mortal. See! I take off my ceremonial beard. *(Removes his spectacle-type beard. Deprecatingly.)* I am now a mortal. *(Relaxes, becoming the interested spectator as he watches the scene between Joseph against Vashnee and Potiphar.)*

JOSEPH. *(Bows to Vashnee.)* The gods of Egypt have zealous servants. They lose no time in gathering their forces.

VASHNEE. *(Returns the bow, then looks at Pharaoh. Speaks charmingly, but with force.)* The gods of Egypt expect all loyal Egyptians to rally to the defense of their temples.

POTIPHAR. Joseph, in my official capacity of All-High Priest of the Sun God and Defender of the Public Faith, I want to ask you a question.

JOSEPH. Please do.

POTIPHAR. Is it true that you are tempting the wrath of the gods by imprisoning the waters of the Nile which they send down every spring in answer to the prayers and sacrifices of our devoted priesthood?

122

JOSEPH. The work begins tomorrow at dawn.

POTIPHAR. This is impossible. It cannot be done.

JOSEPH. Cannot? Why not?

POTIPHAR. The gods will never permit it—never, while the sun rises and the Nile flows.

JOSEPH. *(Studies Pharaoh's face, which remains impassive.)* I'm certain that Pharaoh expects to find the gods highly cooperative with you as the new All-High Priest. Isn't that so, Pharaoh?

PHARAOH. The Pharaoh never meddles with religion. But Joseph, Governor of Egypt, has a free hand.

JOSEPH. *(With satisfaction.)* Thank you, Pharaoh. I knew you would not fail me. *(To Potiphar and Vashnee.)* Eminent All-High Priest and equally eminent High Priestess, if your gods won't be cooperative, see to it that they are supremely indifferent. See to it that they do not interfere with my irrigation project.

POTIPHAR. The gods of Egypt need no human assistance in carrying out their high purpose.

JOSEPH. *(With controlled anger.)* Listen to me, O your Eminences, All-High Priest and High Priestess of the Sun God and Defender of the Public Faith. With your approval or without it, I will build the dams along the Nile. In the midst of this barrenness I will order my engineers to open the doors of my reservoirs. And the water will pour forth exactly where I want it, when I want it and in the quantities I want it. Your priests will pray and say, "Maybe," while my engineers will open doors and keep the fields green. To whom will the people turn when

123

they see that there can be plenty for all, not by prayer but by planning? What will you do then?

PHARAOH. He makes it all seem so simple.

VASHNEE. Does the Pharaoh think that the priesthood will stand by idly while Joseph builds his dams? We have worked too hard and too many centuries to allow him, an infidel and a foreigner, to destroy us. Through our temples we reach into the minds of every Egyptian. What will we tell them about this heresy of imprisonment of the waters of the Holy Nile? How will we instruct them to think? . . . As for the Pharaoh— *(Ritually and with deference.)* —Lord of both lands, loved of Ra, favorite of Mentu, the Lord of Thebes, of Amun and of the Isles of the Sea— *(With force and strength.)* —does the Pharaoh think he can retreat behind the cloak of neutrality? Can the priesthood do anything but look with disfavor if the Pharaoh does not declare himself?

PHARAOH. *(To Joseph.)* It is only a matter of a few hours since I made her High Priestess, and now—

VASHNEE. Once the High Priestess has been ordained, she is from that moment—

PHARAOH. —she presumes to instruct—

VASHNEE. —a force with an independent power of her own.

JOSEPH. You will forever be known as the Pharaoh who abolished hunger from the face of the earth; beneficent as the sun is beneficent, beneficent as the water is beneficent, beneficent as sun and water combined on the land are beneficent—a god in fact and in deed.

PHARAOH. A most appealing prospect.

124

VASHNEE. The Pharaoh will be known as an evil god who brought about civil war. For the priesthood knows how to protect its religious offices. War will be declared against Joseph and his dams. That is the prospect facing the Pharaoh.

PHARAOH. Not so tempting a prospect.

VASHNEE. All this can be avoided quite easily. First, by the Pharaoh declaring himself unequivocally for the priesthood, and second, *(Points to Joseph.)* by discharging this infidel Hebrew from the office of Governor of Egypt.

PHARAOH. So? And whom does the High Priestess have in mind to replace him?

VASHNEE. Malfi. *(Answering Pharaoh's look of incredulity.)* He is stupid and corrupt, but he is safe. *(Preparatory to bowing herself out of Pharaoh's presence.)* May the Pharaoh be worthy of the blessings of the gods, and being worthy, may their blessings be and abide with the Pharaoh, now, henceforth and forever. *(To Potiphar.)* Come, All-High Priest, we will do what it is necessary to do. *(They leave. Pharaoh regards Joseph searchingly for a moment. Then he extracts a hand mirror from his sash and hands it to Joseph to hold. During the next speeches he tries to put on his ceremonial beard, but Joseph deliberately moves the mirror so that he does not succeed in doing so.)*

PHARAOH. *(Admiration creeping into his voice.)* Do you realize that you have just pinched the tail of the Sacred Crocodile of Egypt?

JOSEPH. Egypt can no longer flourish with this holy lie paralyzing her economic system and her brains.

125

PHARAOH. We have managed to live with this lie for thousands of years.

JOSEPH. Are you afraid of the change?

PHARAOH. Of change, no. But of the process of change —perhaps. . . . Stop jiggling the mirror, Joseph.

JOSEPH. Keep that beard off, Pharaoh. Man. Man. Continue to be a man for a while longer. The process of change is a marvelous thing. Don't be afraid of it. Enjoy it.

PHARAOH. Hold your hand steady, Joseph.

JOSEPH. *(His hand still moving.)* Respond to the excitement of the dams and what they can do. *(Pharaoh reaches out his hand to steady Joseph's. Joseph evades Pharaoh's hands.)* The world is always in change; that which does not change is destroyed. . . . When the dams are completed, I plan a Jubilee Year to celebrate the dams and the great Pharaoh who made them possible. *(Turns the face of the sketch and shows it to Pharaoh.)* The Pharaoh who extended the boundaries of his kingdom; the Pharaoh who conquered new lands without war, but with peace. *(Replaces the sketch.)*

PHARAOH. How tempting. How absolutely tempting.

JOSEPH. Do not be afraid of it, Pharaoh. Dare it, Pharaoh. Achieve it, Pharaoh.

PHARAOH. But what of the battle the Sacred Crocodile will put up through her priesthood to retain her powers and privileges?

JOSEPH. You and I together, Pharaoh, we are invincible —even against the Crocodile.

PHARAOH. *(During the following, Pharaoh reaches out*

126

*and holds Joseph's wrist firmly so that the mirror doesn't
move. Pharaoh puts on his ceremonial beard, his body
becoming more erect and kingly. He motions with his
hand for the mirror and replaces it in his sash.)* You amaze
me, Joseph. You have overlooked a major consideration.

JOSEPH. Have I?

PHARAOH. You are prepared to put a project into motion which will jeopardize the priesthood. The priesthood
is aroused and delicately warns me that I would be well
advised to come over to their side, for, in effect, my neutrality gives aid to you. Don't you realize that I could
avoid challenge and threat simply by commanding that all
activities on the dams cease on pain of chopping off your
head? If you had not been so immersed in your project,
you would have seen it for yourself. . . . Less than a year
ago, the All-High Priest—I refer, of course, to the one
who, alas, was assassinated this morning—asked my permission to let him have a temple guard, soldiers whose
duty it would be to guard the temple areas, answerable
only to the All-High Priest. The right to give this permission was mine, but once given could not easily be
withdrawn—this would be an offense to the Sun God
himself. In a moment of mortal error, I, Pharaoh, gave
him that permission. At once he began steadily to build
up an army of his own which soon bid fair to rival mine.
I remonstrated with the All-High Priest, but the temple
guard continued to grow. I understood his intention; it
was to rule Egypt through his temple army. The All-High
Priest was assassinated this morning. There was no other
way. I had planned quite carefully that the sad news of
his untimely end would be brought when Potiphar and

127

Vashnee were having breakfast with me. I had further planned that within minutes Potiphar would be ordained to the office of All-High Priest. I could handle Potiphar without any trouble.

JOSEPH. But you did not forsee that Vashnee would demand the office of High Priestess as the price for allowing Potiphar to become All-High Priest; and thus, your position is not one whit improved. *(Pharaoh nods.)* Pharaoh, join with me. Together we are invincible.

PHARAOH. Perhaps. But then, perhaps not. How can you ask me to take the risk?

JOSEPH. Singlehanded I can't fight the Sacred Crocodile and her army.

PHARAOH. Why not? I give you a free hand.

JOSEPH. But no support.

PHARAOH. None whatever.

JOSEPH. Why? Why?

PHARAOH. All we Pharaohs stay on the safe side.

JOSEPH. If the gods of Egypt were anything but wood and stone they would surely die of laughter.

PHARAOH. Better for the gods to die of laughter than for me to ignore the precedent set by my ancestors.

JOSEPH. *(Goes to side and calls out.)* Call in the engineers and the warrior. *(Walks the room in great perturbation, then goes to desk and studies the plans.)* Prepare to give me your applause.

PHARAOH. I wonder. . . . You can withdraw, you know.

JOSEPH. I cannot turn back.

PHARAOH. You are placing your life in jeopardy, Joseph.

JOSEPH. It is not only my life; it is Egypt's life as well. If *I* don't do it, it will not be done! *(To the two Engineers, and the Warrior who enter.)* Have your messengers already started with the plans?

WARRIOR. They have.

JOSEPH. Then send fast runners after them. We cannot put our entire plan into operation. *(To the two Engineers, pointing.)* This one, your dam Number Four, controls this area as marked? Is that correct?

1ST ENGINEER. Yes.

JOSEPH. Then we will build this single dam—as a trial, as a test, as a proof. But the dam must be completed within five months' time.

1ST ENGINEER. *(In protest.)* Five months. How?

JOSEPH. The men who were to work on the other dams—put them on dam Number Four.

1ST ENGINEER. There is no time to build housing.

JOSEPH. Whatever conditions they have to live under, they will live under—as long as it is necessary.

1ST ENGINEER. And what of their families? There is no time to—

JOSEPH. Move them without their families.

2ND ENGINEER. You can't take them away from their wives and children.

JOSEPH. I can do anything necessary to finish this dam on schedule.

129

1ST ENGINEER. Housing and families are only part of it. We cannot compress enough people into the area to do the work in five months' time.

JOSEPH. I order the work day lengthened. *(Answering the 2nd Engineer's look.)* When the dam is finished they will see that it was done for them.

1ST ENGINEER. Are you prepared for trouble? There could be uprisings.

WARRIOR. Everything will be under control, Excellency. A few whippings have a way of working wonders.

2ND ENGINEER. *(To the Warrior.)* This is not the way we planned it. Whips and beatings were not the basis of this plan.

JOSEPH. *(In an angry shout.)* They will obey or be punished. I am doing it for them. When the dam is completed they can have rest.

2ND ENGINEER. But, Excellency—

JOSEPH. I want results. Go. *(The two Engineers and the Warrior leave.)*

PHARAOH. No proper living quarters; uprooted from their families; an increase of work. You add to the burden of their labors all for some far-distant future. But do they know of this golden future you will so generously bestow upon them?

JOSEPH. *(Stung.)* No. They do not.

PHARAOH. Then perhaps it would be wise to let them in on the secret.

JOSEPH. You leave me no choice but to use force and push ahead. I must be ready by the spring planting. I do not have another year. . . . In ten weeks dam Number Four will be well on the way. Come with me to the site. After you see what I have accomplished you will join forces with me.

PHARAOH. Ten weeks from now—agreed.

JOSEPH. The priests have been pressing for a battle and they shall have it. And, Pharaoh, I promise you an exciting combat.

PHARAOH. When it rages I shall be present, in spirit, cheering for the side that hits the hardest, of course. I admire you, Joseph, and wish you success. But remember, my good wishes will not warp my judgment. When the battle is over, I shall stand beside the victor and share the laurels. That's how my dynasty has endured. *(Turns, starts to go. The lights dim very quickly to be replaced by the blue-green light. In this light Pharaoh and Joseph move off.)*

Scene 3

There is no pause in the action. A spotlight picks up Reuben, the Narrator, as he comes before the audience, playing on his flute. Then he speaks to the audience.

REUBEN. Years ago, Joseph demanded of us, his brothers, that we accept him on faith. He said to us: "You must love me because I am." In answer to this we threw him into the pit. In time he learned that to faith must be added works. But in spite of the fact that he was then able to say, "You must love me because I am and you must love me because my works show that I am mighty"—in spite of this, he was thrown into the pit again and yet once again. Then he stood before the Pharaoh and the Pharaoh raised him from the pit and made him Governor. By then Joseph had learned that to faith and works must be added good intentions. Thus, finally, he was able to say, "You must love me because I am and because I am mighty and because I have good intentions." *(He takes the flute out of his pocket.)* Now you will see what Joseph has still to learn. *(He plays a few notes on the flute.)* Joseph and the Pharaoh started out ten weeks later. They reached the site of dam Number Four. Silence. No work. Joseph

and the Pharaoh quickly made their way to the compound where they found the two engineers and the warrior. *(Joseph, Pharaoh, the two Engineers, the Warrior and a Guard come on stage and take their places. The light on Reuben fades. He moves off the stage. The blue-green light is replaced by the lighting required for the head-quarters in the compound area of the site of dam Number Four.*
It is ten weeks later. The Warrior and the two Engineers are in discussion with Joseph.)

1ST ENGINEER. Then they threw down their sacks and for a long time were silent.

2ND ENGINEER. They did it together, as one man.

WARRIOR. It was planned. I picked one out at random. Flogged him to death. Tore him to pieces with whips. Did it to a second and a third, but they would not move and would not pick up their sacks.

1ST ENGINEER. Excellency, there is a revolt. The work is stopped. Completely stopped. No work of any kind is being done on the dam.

WARRIOR. Three of them, skin torn off their bodies— and suddenly they all broke into a chant.

1ST ENGINEER. *(Sings.)* Who gets the tax
                              That breaks our backs?
(The chant, low and angry, is heard from outside. It is followed by a refrain consisting of one word: "Jo-o-seph!" —bitter and fierce.)

WARRIOR. There it is again.

JOSEPH. Who gets the tax
                 That breaks our backs?

133

(After the refrain, "Jo-o-seph!" he says, shaken.) Joseph! *(The chant and refrain continue as the following goes on.)*

WARRIOR. A battalion. That's all I need. My soldiers will cut them down like barley. A dozen chariots, a hundred spearsmen and a few hundred swordsmen to silence the cries of the wounded. They'll go back to work. Give me permission to order a battalion, Excellency.

2ND ENGINEER. We started work on the dams so that no Egyptian would die of hunger. It was for those people outside. Now he would have his soldiers kill them off.

WARRIOR. I don't care about the dams one way or the other. But once started, this project—or any other project—cannot be stopped. Choke this revolt off, here and now. *(The chant outside dies down. Guard enters, salutes and gives papyrus to 1st Engineer, who reads it and says to Joseph.)*

1ST ENGINEER. Five of them are outside. They claim to be spokesmen for the others. They want to speak to me.

WARRIOR. *(With relish.)* These are the first five I'm going to kill.

JOSEPH. Let them come in. *(The Warrior is about to protest.)* At once. *(Guard goes. Joseph and Pharaoh move off to extreme side where they are hidden by shadows. They wrap their cloaks about them, concealing their insignia of office.)*

PHARAOH. *(To Joseph.)* This is not quite what you led me to believe. Are you sure that your dream of a new Egypt is not a nightmare? I hope you do not fail me, Joseph. I am counting on you to help me against the priesthood. *(Five workers are led in by the Guard. Potiphar and*

Vashnee bring up the rear. They are dressed in ecclesiastical robes but not wearing their ceremonial beards.)

1ST ENGINEER. Why have you thrown down your sacks?

1ST WORKER. We are starved.

2ND WORKER. We are overworked.

1ST WORKER. Work. Work. Work.

3RD WORKER. And when we can work no more, we are whipped by his soldiers.

1ST WORKER. Another day of this and you can feed me to the crocodiles.

2ND WORKER. They wouldn't eat you. Not enough meat.

3RD WORKER. They wouldn't eat any of us.

2ND WORKER. Once only slaves worked as we do, but now free men—

3RD WORKER. Free men? How are we different from the lowest slave?

VASHNEE. *(In this section of the scene she chants liturgically, in a deep voice.)* What do the priests say? *(Joseph and Pharaoh are startled. They move. Vashnee sees them. Pharaoh makes a sign for Vashnee not to reveal Joseph's presence.)*

4TH WORKER. The priests say that the Hebrew foreigner, Joseph, had a god who was strong and ordered everything for Joseph as he wished.

VASHNEE. What more do the priests say?

4TH WORKER. The priests say that the gods of Egypt were weak but now they have become strong again.

135

5TH WORKER. Stronger than the Hebrew god.

VASHNEE. What more do the priests say?

4TH WORKER. The priests say Joseph is demon. He should be killed.

VASHNEE. Repeat.

3RD, 4TH and 5TH WORKERS. *(Together.)* The priests say Joseph is demon. He should be killed.

JOSEPH. *(Springs out of the shadows.)* You are working for your own good and the good of your children.

1ST WORKER. *(Derisively.)* My own good. Till Joseph came along I had my fields of corn and barley. Look at me now.

2ND WORKER. Till Joseph came along I lived with my wife and babes. Look at me now.

3RD WORKER. One day the soldiers came and dragged me off to the work camps. Look at me now.

1ST WORKER. Look at us. Look at us.

4TH WORKER. Who are you?

JOSEPH. I am Joseph.

THE WORKERS. Joseph!

JOSEPH. Yes, Joseph. Everything I have done is for the good of Egypt.

2ND WORKER. How? By working us to death?

JOSEPH. *(Though Joseph delivers the following speech in full, only the beginning is heard. The rest is drowned out, except for a few words or a phrase here and there. At*

136

first there is unrest, which turns to anger, then heckling. After two or three sentences of Joseph's speech, the First Worker calls out: "Shut his mouth." Then the Third Worker calls out: "Silence him." After another sentence or two, the Fourth Worker begins chanting: "Yo. Yo. Yo. Yo." The others follow suit, drowning out Joseph's words. Then the Fifth Worker starts chanting: "Hoo. Hoo. Hoo. Hoo." The others join in. Then the Third Worker shouts directly to Joseph: "If you're not quiet, I'll kill you." He starts to advance on Joseph, the others following him. The Warrior and the Guard move toward the Workers. Joseph stands his ground and continues.) The dams will forever free Egypt from drought and famine. But the priests say the water must stay in the hands of the gods because they have made the farmer in the field, the merchant in the city and the cowherd on the plains believe that the gods make the waters of the Nile flow *only* in answer to their prayers and sacrifices. If the water doesn't rise high enough, or if the water rises too high, it's because you people of Egypt haven't prayed and sacrificed enough. So you pinch and scrape and save. A little gold from one, a cow from another, a dozen measures of corn from a third. Something from every pious Egyptian, no matter how poor. And who gets it? It flows into the coffers of the temples and from there into the pockets of the priesthood. The dams will take the water out of the hands of the priesthood and give it back into your hands. *(The situation is difficult; it is just on the edge of getting out of hand.)*

PHARAOH. *(Steps forward out of the shadows. Regally.)* Hail, sons of Egypt!

2ND WORKER. *(Astonished.)* Who are you?

137

ACT II

PHARAOH. *(Opens his enveloping cloak, revealing his royal dress.)*
I am Pharaoh, anointed of Isis.
(Ritualistically.)
I am he who is and shall be father to the orphans,
I am he who is and shall be everlasting husband to the widow,
I am brother to the desolate woman,
The garment to the motherless.
I am he who raises up every good thing and crushes evil.
(In normal tones, warmly and sympathetically.)
Sons of Egypt, you are my children. I have come to see if all is well with you.

1ST WORKER. Hail, Pharaoh! All is not well with us.

2ND WORKER. We have been forsaken.

3RD WORKER. We die without hope, like flies.

PHARAOH. Why have you not told me this before?

2ND WORKER. You are so far away. Our voices could not reach you.

1ST WORKER. The priests have said you sold us as slaves to the Hebrew for taxes.

PHARAOH. The true father of Egypt does not sell his children. *(In Vashnee's direction.)* And I am surprised at the priests for saying such a thing without first consulting me.

4TH WORKER. Then you will save us, Pharaoh? We will no longer be slaves to that Hebrew, Joseph?

PHARAOH. From this moment you are free men. You shall be returned to your families.

SCENE 3

ALL THE WORKERS. *(Shouting.)* Free men!
(They murmur.)
May the gods send Pharaoh long life.
May the gods reward you.
Oh, good Pharaoh.
Pharaoh, great and good.

PHARAOH. Are you content now? If you are not content, ask what you wish. Pharaoh will grant it.

4TH WORKER. Pharaoh will grant whatever we ask?

PHARAOH. Yes.

4TH WORKER. Then kill Joseph!

3RD WORKER. Kill Joseph.

THE WORKERS. *(All.)* Kill Joseph. Kill Joseph. Kill Joseph. *(The cry is taken up outside the tent.)*

PHARAOH. *(Raising his hand.)* Enough. *(There is absolute silence.)* Joseph shall die.

4TH WORKER. When? *(Pharaoh does not answer.)*

2ND WORKER. Tonight? *(Pharaoh looks at him with a mask-like expression.)*

3RD WORKER. Tomorrow? *(Pharaoh's expression remains unchanged.)*

VASHNEE. The Pharaoh will decide on the time and the place—with the help of the priests. Go now.

WARRIOR. High Priestess, I am at your service. *(The Workers, the Two Engineers, the Warrior and the Guard back out of Pharaoh's presence.)*

VASHNEE. *(To Potiphar.)* Go with them, All-High Priest, and see that nothing gets out of hand.

139

POTIPHAR. You are right, High Priestess. At once. *(Potiphar leaves.)*

JOSEPH. Pharaoh, what have you done?

VASHNEE. What you have seen tonight will soon be duplicated everywhere. I can make uprisings like this one spread over the breadth of Egypt.

PHARAOH. And when they do, even I will not be safe.

JOSEPH. So, therefore, you kill me.

PHARAOH. Kill you? Not at all. I promised them only that you should die. So shall we all—at our appointed time. Meanwhile, if Vashnee is agreeable, you may join Arraffi restfully in the desert.

VASHNEE. We shall appoint Malfi in your place.

PHARAOH. *(Answering Joseph's horrified look.)* Were I to side with you I would lose my throne.

JOSEPH. You have lost your throne. You are presiding at the death of Egypt. To be a Pharaoh today, you must be a man. And you are less than a man, and less than a Pharaoh. Change. Change. Change. Vashnee wants nothing to change in Egypt; the priesthood wants nothing to change. They can live without change. But Egypt cannot live without change and you cannot live without change. Egypt will crumble. You are the destroyer.

PHARAOH. Do not grieve, Joseph.

JOSEPH. It is not for myself that I grieve. I grieve that I have failed—

PHARAOH. Failed to find men ready to sacrifice themselves for future generations? I don't want to do it. Nor do my people. They want to bask in the sun, dance under the full moon and make love in their gardens. They are not heroes.

JOSEPH. It is you who wants to bask in the sun; it is you who wants to dance under the full moon; it is you who wants to make love in your gardens; it is you who is not a hero. As for the people, they may not be heroes, but they have the instinct to free themselves. That makes heroes. I gave them slavery and their instinct told them that a touch of freedom is better than slavery. *(To Vashnee.)* You tricked and seduced them— *(To Pharaoh.)* —and you joined in the betrayal. But their instinct for freedom is true. This cannot be denied.

PHARAOH. *(With a sharp undertone.)* Call a halt, Joseph, call a halt to these ramblings. Your fabulous imagination is playing you false.

JOSEPH. No. My imagination was not great enough. I thought that the only way I could succeed was to work apart, alone, and give them a perfected finished state. I have squandered my days of power and betrayed them into Vashnee's hands and yours. *(As a question, very tentatively, not at all sure of the answer.)* Could I have taught the people to put their faith in one another and not in the deceptive power of rulers or in the false promises of priests? Would these men then have been ready to walk with me through the dark night of Egypt's travail? *(With increasing vigor and affirmation.)* Pharaoh, if that time ever comes, the gods and their superstitions, the tyrants and their slavery will vanish. For these men will be heroes, and heroes need no gods and no tyrants.

PHARAOH. I am not concerned, O Prophet, if the day comes when men will become heroes ready to sacrifice

141

themselves for the future, for surely by that time I shall be as comfortably dead as you.

VASHNEE. And as for me, O Prophet, these abstract speculations are exceedingly interesting, but as a practical politician, my only concern is with the present.

PHARAOH. Go now. The desert waits for you. . . . But let me give you some words of comfort. You have done as much as any man can do in his time. The dams will be built. Rest content in that knowledge. But it will take a longer time than you thought.

JOSEPH. The dams could be built in my generation.

PHARAOH. I see that Arraffi will have to teach you patience. (*Joseph loosens his enveloping cloak. He takes off the official outer robe of the Governor of Egypt and flings it at Pharaoh's feet. Then he takes off the golden collar of the Governor of Egypt and flings it at Pharaoh's feet. Now he is in his underdress, a dark tunic of rough-looking material, suggestive of the tunic he wore when the brothers stripped him of the coat of many colors, and suggestive also of Arraffi's desert garb.*)

VASHNEE. (*Off to one side, calls out softly.*) Send in my two men.

JOSEPH. I am thrown into the pit again—for the desert is as the pit. But I shall rise out of the pit once more and return. Whatever it is I must learn, I *will* learn. I shall return. Until then— (*Spreads out his arms wide and in a great voice, cries out.*) Egypt, Egypt, farewell. I leave you to your gods and to your tyrants. (*He moves out of Pharaoh's and Vashnee's presence and disappears. Two armed Mercenaries enter.*)

142

SCENE 3

PHARAOH. No, Vashnee.

VASHNEE. There is a man going into the desert. Wait until he is a good distance in it, then fall on him. Do not bury him. Let buzzards feed on his flesh. Let nothing remain but his white bones on the desert floor. Let nothing distinguish him from any other unfortunate traveler. *(The Two Mercenaries nod their heads with understanding and go out swiftly.)*

PHARAOH. Call them back. I have banished him into the desert. He will not bother you again.

VASHNEE. Be silent. I did not ask you. Do you think I will give him the opportunity to rise from the pit once again? To be banished into the desert is not to die; to die is to die. This time he will go down into the pit and remain there. *(Pharaoh turns his back; He is bent and cowering. He covers his entire body, including head and face, with his large cloak so that nothing shows but the outline of his figure, suggesting perhaps a shrunken mummy. Vashnee takes an immobile position, suggesting a statue. The light has been fading.)*

THE END